IN THIS PEPPERY—OFTEN STARTLING — VIEW OF THE CONTEMPORARY AMERICAN SCENE THE SINGULAR MISS MCCARTHY SPEAKS HER MIND:

"When an American heiress wants to buy a man, she at once crosses the Atlantic. The only really materialistic people I have ever met have been Europeans."

"Every age has a keyhole to which its eye is pasted. . . . In our own day, this type of sensational fact-fiction is being produced largely by ex-Communists. Public curiosity shows an almost prurient avidity for the details of political defloration, and the memoirs of ex-Communists have an odd resemblance to the confessions of a white slave."

"Throughout Miller's long practice as a realist, there is not only a naïve searching for another dimension but an evident hatred of and contempt for reality—as not good enough to make plays out of. It is natural, therefore, that he should never have any interest in how people talk; his characters all talk the same way—somewhat funereally, through their noses."

"If psychoanalysis has a cure for [frigidity] . . . this must be the best-kept medical secret of modern times . . ."

"Miss McCarthy's well-known qualities — wit, style, audacity, and force of intellect—are very much in evidence . . . a spirited and distinguished collection of essays."—*The Atlantic*

Other SIGNET Books by Mary McCarthy

CAST A COLD EYE
Sharply etched short stories by one of America's finest satirists, author of *The Group*. The book also includes a short novel, *The Oasis*, which has long been out of print. (#T2380—75¢)

A CHARMED LIFE
A worldly, vivid novel about the inhabitants of an artist's colony in a bleak New England seacoast town. (#T2416—75¢)

THE GROVES OF ACADEME
A satiric novel of scandal and subterfuge in a progressive New England college by the writer whom the *Saturday Review* has called "one of the most stunning talents today." (#T2372—75¢)

To Our Readers

We welcome your request for our free catalog of SIGNET and MENTOR books. If your dealer does not have the books you want, you may order them by mail, enclosing the list price plus 5¢ a copy to cover mailing. The New American Library of World Literature, Inc., P. O. Box 2310, Grand Central Station, New York, New York 10017.

MARY MCCARTHY

The Humanist in the Bathtub

Selected Essays from Mary McCarthys'
Theatre Chronicles 1937-1962
and On the Contrary

A SIGNET BOOK published by
The New American Library

Published as a SIGNET BOOK
by arrangement with Farrar, Straus and Company, Inc., who have authorized this softcover edition.

FIRST PRINTING, JUNE, 1964

"America the Beautiful: The Humanist in the Bathtub" originally appeared in *Commentary;* "A New Word" in *Harper's Bazaar;* "Artists in Uniform" and "Settling the Colonel's Hash" in *Harper's Magazine;* "The American Realist Playwrights" in *Harper's Magazine* and *Encounter;* "The Vassar Girl" in *Holiday;* "Tyranny of the Orgasm" in the *New Leader;* "An Academy of Risk," "Characters in Fiction," "Drapes," "The Fact in Fiction" and "Odd Man In" in *Partisan Review;* "Mlle. Gulliver en Amérique" in *The Reporter;* "My Confession" in *The Reporter* and *Encounter.*

"A New Word," "Odd Man In," and "Drapes" are from *Theatre Chronicles.* All other essays are from *On the Contrary.*

SIGNET BOOKS are published by
The New American Library of World Publishing, Inc.
501 Madison Avenue, New York, New York 10022

PRINTED IN THE UNITED STATES OF AMERICA

Contents

America the Beautiful

THE HUMANIST IN THE BATHTUB

A visiting Existentialist wanted recently to be taken to dinner at a really American place. This proposal, natural enough in a tourist, disclosed a situation thoroughly unnatural. Unless the visiting lady's object was suffering, there was no way of satisfying her demand. Sukiyaki joints, chop suey joints, Italian table d'hôte places, French provincial restaurants with the menu written on a slate, Irish chophouses, and Jewish delicatessens came abundantly to mind, but these were not what the lady wanted. Schrafft's or the Automat would have answered, yet to take her there would have been to turn oneself into a tourist and to present America as a spectacle—a *New Yorker* cartoon or a savage drawing in the *New Masses*. It was the beginning of an evening of humiliations. The visitor was lively and eager; her mind lay open and orderly, like a notebook ready for impressions. It was not long, however, before she shut it up with a snap. We had no recommendations to make to her. With movies, plays, current books, it was the same story as with the restaurants. *Open City, Les Enfants du Paradis,* Oscar Wilde, a reprint of Henry James were *paté de maison* to this lady who wanted the definitive flapjack. She did not believe us when we said that there were no good Hollywood movies, no good Broadway plays—only curios; she was merely confirmed in her impression that American intellectuals were "negative."

7

Yet the irritating thing was that we did not feel negative. We admired and liked our country; we preferred it to that imaginary America, land of the *peaux rouges* of Caldwell and Steinbeck, dumb paradise of violence and the detective story, which had excited the sensibilities of our visitor and of the up-to-date French literary world. But to found our preference, to locate it materially in some admirable object or institution, such as Chartres, say, or French café life, was for us, that night at any rate, an impossible undertaking. We heard ourselves saying that the real America was elsewhere, in the white frame houses and church spires of New England; yet we knew that we talked foolishly—we were not Granville Hicks and we looked ludicrous in his opinions. The Elevated, half a block away, interrupting us every time a train passed, gave us the lie on schedule, every eight minutes. But if the elm-shaded village green was a false or at least an insufficient address for the *genius loci* we honored, where then was it to be found? Surveyed from the vantage point of Europe, this large continent seemed suddenly deficient in objects of virtue. The Grand Canyon, Yellowstone Park, Jim Hill's mansion in St. Paul, Jefferson's Monticello, the blast furnaces of Pittsburgh, Mount Rainier, the yellow observatory at Amherst, the little-theatre movement in Cleveland, Ohio, a Greek revival house glimpsed from a car window in a lost river-town in New Jersey—these things were too small for the size of the country. Each of them, when pointed to, diminished in interest with the lady's perspective of distance. There was no sight that in itself seemed to justify her crossing of the Atlantic.

If she was interested in "conditions," that was a different matter. There are conditions everywhere; it takes no special genius to produce them. Yet would it be an act of hospitality to invite a visitor to a lynching? Unfortunately, nearly all the "sights" in America fall under the head of conditions. Hollywood, Reno, the sharecroppers' homes in the South, the mining towns of Pennsylvania, Coney Island, the Chicago stockyards, Macy's, the Dodgers, Harlem, even Congress, the forum of our liberties, are spectacles rather than sights, to use the term in the colloquial sense of "Didn't he make a holy spectacle of himself?" An Englishman of almost any political opinion can show a visitor through the houses of Parliament with a sense of pride or at least of indulgence toward his national foibles and traditions. The American, if he has a spark of national feeling, will be humiliated by the very prospect of a foreigner's visit to Congress—these, for the most part, illiterate hacks whose fancy vests are spotted with gravy, and whose speeches, hypocritical, unctuous, and slovenly, are spotted also with the gravy of political patronage, these persons are a reflection on the democratic process rather than of it; they expose it in its underwear. In European legislation, we are told, a great deal of shady business goes on in private, behind the scenes. In America, it is just the opposite, anything good, presumably, is accomplished *in camera,* in the committee rooms.

It is so with all our institutions. For the visiting European, a trip through the United States has, almost inevitably, the character of an exposé, and the American, on his side, is tempted by love of his country to lock the inquiring tourist in his hotel room and throw away the key. His contention that the visible and material America is not the real or the only one is more difficult to sustain than was the presumption of the "other" Germany behind the Nazi steel.

To some extent a citizen of any country will feel that the tourist's view of his homeland is a false one. The French will tell you that you have to go into their homes to see what the French people are really like. The intellectuals in the Left Bank cafés are not the real French intellectuals, etc., etc. In Italy, they complain that the tourist must not judge by the *ristorantes;* there one sees only black-market types. But in neither of these cases is the native really disturbed by the tourist's view of his country. If Versailles or Giotto's bell-tower in Florence

do not tell the whole story, they are still not incongruous
with it; you do not hear a Frenchman or an Italian object when these things are noticed by a visitor. With the
American, the contradiction is more serious. He must, if
he is to defend his country, repudiate its visible aspect
almost entirely. He must say that its parade of phenome-
nology, its billboards, super-highways, even its skyscrapers, not only fail to represent the inner essence of
his country but in fact contravene it. He may point, if
he wishes, to certain beautiful objects, but here too he is
in difficulties, for nearly everything that is beautiful and
has not been produced by Nature belongs to the eighteenth
century, to a past with which he has very little connection,
and which his ancestors, in many or most cases, had no
part in. Beacon Street and the Boston Common are very
charming in the eighteenth-century manner, so are the
sea captains' houses in the old Massachusetts ports, and
the ruined plantations of Louisiana, but an American from
Brooklyn or the Middle West or the Pacific Coast finds
the style of life embodied in them as foreign as Europe;
indeed, the first sensation of a Westerner, coming upon
Beacon Hill and the gold dome of the State House, is to
feel that at last he has traveled "abroad." The American,
if he is to speak the highest truth about his country,
must refrain from pointing at all. The virtue of American
civilization is that it is unmaterialistic.

This statement may strike a critic as whimsical or per-
verse. Everybody knows, it will be said, that America has
the most materialistic civilization in the world, that Americans care only about money, they have no time or talent
for living; look at radio, look at advertising, look at life
insurance, look at the tired business man, at the Frigidaires and the Fords. In answer, the reader is invited
first to look instead into his own heart and inquire
whether he personally feels himself to be represented by
these things, or whether he does not, on the contrary,
feel them to be irrelevant to him, a necessary evil, part
of the conditions of life. Other people, he will assume,
care about them very much: the man down the street,

the entire population of Detroit or Scarsdale, the back-country farmer, the urban poor or the rich. But he himself accepts these objects as imposed on him by a collective "otherness" of desire, an otherness he has not met directly but whose existence he infers from the number of automobiles, Frigidaires, or television sets he sees around him. Stepping into his new Buick convertible, he knows that he would gladly do without it, but imagines that to his neighbor, who is just backing *his* out of the driveway, this car is the motor of life. More often, however, the otherness is projected farther afield, onto a different class or social group, remote and alien. Thus the rich, who would like nothing better, they think, than for life to be a perpetual fishing trip with the trout grilled by a native guide, look patronizingly upon the whole apparatus of American civilization as a cheap Christmas present to the poor, and city people see the radio and the washing machine as the farm-wife's solace.

It can be argued, of course, that the subjective view is prevaricating, possession of the Buick being nine-tenths of the social law. But who has ever met, outside of advertisements, a true parishioner of this church of Mammon? A man may take pride in a car, and a housewife in her new sink or wallpaper, but pleasure in new acquisitions is universal and eternal; an Italian man with a new gold tooth, a French bibliophile with a new edition, a woman with a new baby, a philosopher with a new thought, all these people are rejoicing in progress, in man's power to enlarge and improve. Before men showed off new cars, they showed off new horses; it is alleged against modern man that he as an individual craftsman did not make the car; but his grandfather did not make the horse either. What is imputed to Americans is something quite different, an abject dependence on material possessions, an image of happiness as packaged by the manufacturer, content in a can. This view of American life is strongly urged by advertising agencies. We know the "others," of course, because we meet them every week in full force

in *The New Yorker* or the *Saturday Evening Post,* those
brightly colored families of dedicated consumers, waiting
in unison on the porch for the dealer to deliver the new
car, gobbling the new cereal ("Gee, Mom, is it good for
you too?"), lining up to bank their paychecks, or fear-
fully anticipating the industrial accident and the insurance-
check that will "compensate" for it. We meet them also,
more troll-like underground, in the subway placards, in
the ferociously complacent One-A-Day family, and we hear
their courtiers sing to them on the radio of Ivory or
Supersuds. The thing, however, that repels us in these advertisements is their naïve falsity to life. Who are these
advertising men kidding, besides the European tourist?
Between the tired, sad, gentle faces of the subway riders
and the grinning Holy Families of the Ad-Mass, there
exists no possibility of even a wishful identification. We
take a vitamin pill with the hope of feeling (possibly) a
little less tired, but the superstition of buoyant health em-
blazoned in the bright, ugly pictures has no more power
to move us than the blood of St. Januarius.

Familiarity has perhaps bred contempt in us Americans:
until you have had a washing machine, you cannot imagine
how little difference it will make to you. Europeans still
believe that money brings happiness, witness the bought
journalist, the bought politician, the bought general, the
whole venality of European literary life, inconceivable in
this country of the dollar. It is true that America pro-
duces and consumes more cars, soap, and bathtubs than
any other nation, but we live among these objects rather
than by them. Americans build skyscrapers; Le Corbusier
worships them. Ehrenburg, our Soviet critic, fell in love
with the Check-O-Mat in American railway stations, writing home paragraphs of song to this gadget—while deploring American materialism. When an American heiress
wants to buy a man, she at once crosses the Atlantic.
The only really materialistic people I have ever met have
been Europeans.

The strongest argument for the un-materialistic character of American life is the fact that we tolerate condi-

tions that are, from a materialistic point of view, intolerable. What the foreigner finds most objectionable in American life is its lack of basic comfort. No nation with any sense of material well-being would endure the food we eat, the cramped apartments we live in, the noise, the traffic, the crowded subways and buses. American life, in large cities, at any rate, is a perpetual assault on the senses and the nerves; it is out of asceticism, out of unworldliness, precisely, that we bear it.

This republic was founded on an unworldly assumption, a denial of "the facts of life." It is manifestly untrue that all men are created equal; interpreted in worldly terms, this doctrine has resulted in a pseudo-equality, that is, in standardization, in an equality of things rather than of persons. The inalienable rights to life, liberty, and the pursuit of happiness appear, in practice, to have become the inalienable right to a bathtub, a flush toilet, and a can of Spam. Left-wing critics of America attribute this result to the intrusion of capitalism; right-wing critics see it as the logical dead end of democracy. Capitalism, certainly, now depends on mass production, which depends on large-scale distribution of uniform goods, till the consumer today is the victim of the manufacturer who launches on him a regiment of products for which he must make house-room in his soul. The buying impulse, in its original force and purity, was not nearly so crass, however, or so meanly acquisitive as many radical critics suppose. The purchase of a bathtub was the exercise of a spiritual right. The immigrant or the poor native American bought a bathtub, not because he wanted to take a bath, but because he wanted to be in a *position* to do so. This remains true in many fields today; possessions, when they are desired, are not wanted for their own sakes but as tokens of an ideal state of freedom, fraternity, and franchise. "Keeping up with the Joneses" is a vulgarization of Jefferson's concept, but it too is a declaration of the rights of man, and decidedly unfeasible and visionary. Where for a European, a fact is a fact, for us Americans, the real, if it is relevant at all, is simply symbolic appearance. We are a nation of twenty million bathrooms, with a humanist in every tub. One such humanist I used to hear of on Cape Cod had, on growing rich, installed two toilets side by side in his marble bathroom, on the model of the two-seater of his youth. He was a clear case of Americanism, hospitable, gregarious, and impractical, a theorist of perfection. Was his dream of the conquest of poverty a vulgar dream or a noble one, a material demand or a spiritual insistence? It is hard to think of him as a happy man, and in this too he is characteristically American, for the parity of the radio, the movies, and the washing machine has made Americans sad, reminding them of another parity of which these things were to be but emblems.

The American does not enjoy his possessions because sensory enjoyment was not his object, and he lives sparely and thinly among them, in the monastic discipline of Scarsdale or the barracks of Stuyvesant Town. Only among certain groups where franchise, socially speaking, has not been achieved, do pleasure and material splendor constitute a life-object and an occupation. Among the outcasts—Jews, Negroes, Catholics, homosexuals—excluded from the communion of ascetics, the love of fabrics, gaudy show, and rich possessions still anachronistically flaunts itself. Once a norm has been reached, differing in the different classes, financial ambition itself seems to fade away. The self-made man finds, to his anger, his son uninterested in money; you have shirtsleeves to shirtsleeves in three generations. The great financial empires are a thing of the past. Some recent immigrants—movie magnates and gangsters particularly—retain their acquisitiveness, but how long is it since anyone in the general public has murmured, wonderingly, "as rich as Rockefeller"?

If the dream of American fraternity had ended simply in this, the value of humanistic and egalitarian strivings would be seriously called into question. Jefferson, the Adamses, Franklin, Madison, would be in the position of

Dostoevsky's Grand Inquisitor, who, desiring to make the Kingdom of God incarnate on earth, inaugurated the kingdom of the devil. If the nature of matter is such that the earthly paradise, once realized, becomes always the paradise of the earthly, and a spiritual conquest of matter becomes an enslavement of spirit, then the atomic bomb is, as has been argued, the logical result of the Enlightenment, and the land of opportunity is, precisely, the land of death. This position, however, is a strictly materialist one, for it asserts the Fact of the bomb as the one tremendous truth: subjective attitudes are irrelevant; it does not matter what we think or feel; possession again in this case is nine-tenths of the law.

It must be admitted that there is a great similarity between the nation with its new bomb and the consumer with his new Buick. In both cases, there is a disinclination to use the product, stronger naturally in the case of the bomb, but somebody has manufactured the thing, and there seems to be no way *not* to use it, especially when everybody else will be doing so. Here again the argument of the "others" is invoked to justify our own procedures: if we had not invented the bomb, the Germans would have; the Soviet Union will have it in a year, etc., etc. This is keeping up with the Joneses indeed, our national propagandists playing the role of the advertising men in persuading us of the "others' " intentions.

It seems likely at this moment that we will find no way of not using the bomb, yet those who argue theoretically that this machine is the true expression of our society leave us, in practice, with no means of opposing it. We must differentiate ourselves from the bomb if we are to avoid using it, and in private thought we do, distinguishing the bomb sharply from our daily concerns and sentiments, feeling it as an otherness that waits outside to descend on us, an otherness already destructive of normal life, since it prevents us from planning or hoping by depriving us of a future. And this inner refusal of the bomb is also a legacy of our past; it is a denial of the given, of the power of circumstances to shape us in their mold.

Unfortunately, the whole asceticism of our national character, our habit of living in but not through an environment, our alienation from objects, prepare us to endure the bomb but not to confront it.

Passivity and not aggressiveness is the dominant trait of the American character. The movies, the radio, the super-highway have softened us up for the atom bomb; we have lived with them without pleasure, feeling them as a coercion on our natures, a coercion seemingly from nowhere and expressing nobody's will. The new coercion finds us without the habit of protest; we are dissident but apart.

The very "negativeness," then, of American intellectuals is not a mark of their separation from our society, but a true expression of its separation from itself. We too are dissident but inactive. Intransigent on paper, in "real life" we conform; yet we do not feel ourselves to be dishonest, for to us the real life is rustling paper and the mental life is flesh. And even in our mental life we are critical and rather unproductive; we leave it to the "others," the best-sellers, to create.

The fluctuating character of American life must, in part, have been responsible for this dissociated condition. Many an immigrant arrived in this country with the most materialistic expectations, hoping, not to escape from a world in which a man was the sum of his circumstances, but to become a new sum of circumstances himself. But this hope was self-defeating; the very ease with which new circumstances were acquired left insufficient time for a man to live into them: all along a great avenue in Minneapolis the huge stone chateaux used to be dark at night, save for a single light in each kitchen, where the family still sat, Swedish-style, about the stove. The pressure of democratic thought, moreover, forced a rising man often, unexpectedly, to recognize that he was *not* his position: a speeding ticket from a village constable could lay him low. Like the agitated United Nations delegates who got summonses on the Merritt Parkway, he might find the shock traumatic: a belief had been destroyed. The effect of these combined difficulties turned the new American into a nomad, who camped out in his circumstances, as it were, and was never assimilated to them. And, for the native American, the great waves of internal migration had the same result. The homelessness of the American, migrant in geography and on the map of finance, is the whole subject of the American realists of our period. European readers see in these writers only violence and brutality. They miss not only the pathos but the nomadic virtues associated with it, generosity, hospitality, equity, directness, politeness, simplicity of relations—traits which, together with a certain gentle timidity (as of very *unpracticed* nomads), comprise the American character. Unobserved also is a peculiar nakedness, a look of being shorn of everything, that is very curiously American, corresponding to the spare wooden desolation of a frontier town and the bright thinness of the American light. The American character looks always as if it had just had a rather bad haircut, which gives it, in our eyes at any rate, a greater humanity than the European, which even among its beggars has an all too professional air.

The openness of the American situation creates the pity and the terror; status is not protection; life for the European is a career; for the American, it is a hazard. Slaves and women, said Aristotle, are not fit subjects for tragedy, but kings, rather, and noble men, men, that is, not defined by circumstance but outside it and seemingly impervious. In America we have, subjectively speaking, no slaves and no women; the efforts of *PM* and the Stalinized playwrights to introduce, like the first step to servitude, a national psychology of the "little man" have been, so far, unrewarding. The little man is one who is embedded in status; things can be done for and to him generically by a central directive; his happiness flows from statistics. This conception mistakes the national passivity for abjection. Americans will not eat this humble pie; we are still nature's noblemen. Yet no tragedy results, though the protagonist is everywhere; dissociation takes the place of conflict, and the drama is mute.

This humanity, this plain and heroic accessibility, was what we would have liked to point out to the visiting Existentialist as our national glory. Modesty perhaps forbade and a lack of concrete examples—how could we point to ourselves? Had we done so she would not have been interested. To a European, the humanity of an intellectual is of no particular moment; it is the barber pole that announces his profession and the hair oil dispensed inside. Europeans, moreover, have no curiosity about American intellectuals; we are insufficiently representative of the brute. Yet this anticipated and felt disparagement was not the whole cause of our reticence. We were silent for another reason: we were waiting to be discovered. Columbus, however, passed on, and this, very likely, was the true source of our humiliation. But this experience also was peculiarly American. We all expect to be found in the murk of otherness; it looks to us very easy since *we* know we are there. Time after time, the explorers have failed to see us. We have been patient, for the happy ending is our national belief. Now, however, that the future has been shut off from us, it is necessary for us to declare ourselves, at least for the record.

What it amounts to, in verity, is that we are the poor. This humanity we would claim for ourselves is the legacy, not only of the Enlightenment, but of the thousands and thousands of European peasants and poor townspeople who came here bringing their humanity and their sufferings with them. It is the absence of a stable upper class that is responsible for much of the vulgarity of the American scene. Should we blush before the visitor for this deficiency? The ugliness of American decoration, American entertainment, American literature—is not this the visible expression of the impoverishment of the European masses, a manifestation of all the backwardness, deprivation, and want that arrived here in boatloads from Europe? The immense popularity of American movies abroad demonstrates that Europe is the unfinished negative of which America is the proof. The European traveler, viewing with distaste a movie palace or a Motorola, is only looking into the terrible concavity of his continent of hunger inverted startlingly into the convex. Our civilization, deformed as it is outwardly, is still an accomplishment; all this had to come to light.

America is indeed a revelation, though not quite the one that was planned. Given a clean slate, man, it was hoped, would write the future. Instead, he has written his past. This past, inscribed on billboards, ball parks, dance halls, is not seemly, yet its objectification is a kind of disburdenment. The past is at length outside. It does not disturb us as it does Europeans, for our relation with it is both more distant and more familiar. We cannot hate it, for to hate it would be to hate poverty, our eager ancestors, and ourselves.

If there were time, American civilization could be seen as a beginning, even a favorable one, for we have only to look around us to see what a lot of sensibility a little ease will accrue. The children surpass the fathers and Louis B. Mayer cannot be preserved intact in his descendants. . . . Unfortunately, as things seem now, posterity is not around the corner.

September, 1947

Mlle. Gulliver en Amérique

In January, 1947, Simone de Beauvoir, the leading French *femme savante,* alighted from an airplane at La-Guardia Field for a four months' stay in the United States. In her own eyes, this trip had something fabulous about it, of a balloonist's expedition or a descent in a diving bell. Where to Frenchmen of an earlier generation, America was the incredible country of *les peaux rouges* and the novels of Fenimore Cooper, to Mlle. de Beauvoir America was, very simply, movieland—she came to verify for herself the existence of violence, drugstore stools, boy-meets-girl, that she had seen depicted on the screen. Her impressions, which she set down in journal form for the readers of *Les Temps Modernes,* retained therefore the flavor of an eyewitness account, of confirmation of rumor, the object being not so much to assay America as to testify to its reality.

These impressions, collected into a book, made a certain stir in France; now, three years later, they are appearing in translation in Germany. The book has never been published over here; the few snatches excerpted from it in magazine articles provoked wonder and hostility.

On an American leafing through the pages of an old library copy, the book has a strange effect. It is as though an inhabitant of Lilliput or Brobdingnag, coming

upon a copy of *Gulliver's Travels,* sat down to read, in a
foreign tongue, of his own local customs codified by an
observer of a different species: everything is at once
familiar and distorted. The landmarks are there, and
some of the institutions and personages—Eighth Avenue,
Broadway, Hollywood, the Grand Canyon, Harvard, Yale,
Vassar, literary celebrities concealed under initials; here
are the drugstores and the cafeterias and the busses and
the traffic lights—and yet it is all wrong, schematized,
rationalized, like a scale model under glass. Peering down
at himself, the American discovers that he has "no sense
of *nuance,*" that he is always in a good humor, that "in
America the individual is nothing," that all Americans
think their native town is the most beautiful town in the
world, that an office girl cannot go to work in the same
dress two days running, that in hotels "illicit" couples are
made to swear that they are married, that it almost never
happens here that a professor is also a writer, that the
majority of American novelists have never been to college, that the middle class has no hold on the country's
economic life and very little influence on its political
destiny, that the good American citizen is never sick,
that racism and reaction grow more menacing every day,
that "the appearance, even, of democracy is vanishing
from day to day," and that the country is witnessing
"the birth of fascism."

From these pages, he discovers, in short, that his
country has become, in the eyes of Existentialists, a future which is, so to speak, already a past, a gelid eternity
of drugstores, juke boxes, smiles, refrigerators, and
"fascism," and that he himself is no longer an individual
but a sort of Mars man, a projection of science fiction, the
man of 1984. Such a futuristic vision of America was
already in Mlle. de Beauvoir's head when she descended
from the plane as from a space ship, wearing metaphorical
goggles: eager as a little girl to taste the rock-candy de-
lights of this materialistic moon civilization (the orange
juice, the ice creams, the jazz, the whiskeys, the martinis, and the lobster). She knows already, nevertheless,

that this world is not "real," but only a half-frightening fantasy daydreamed by the Americans.

She has preserved enough of Marxism to be warned that the spun-sugar façade is a device of the "Pullman class" to mask its exploitation and cruelty: while the soda fountains spout, Truman and Marshall prepare an anti-Communist crusade that brings back memories of the Nazis, and Congress plots the ruin of the trade unions. "The collective future is in the hands of a privileged class, the Pullman class, to which are reserved the joys of large-scale enterprise and creation; the others are just wheels in a big steel world; they lack the power to conceive an individual future for themselves; they have no plan or passion, hope or nostalgia, that carries them beyond the present; they know only the unending repetition of the cycle of seasons and hours."

This image of a people from Oz or out of an expressionist ballet, a robot people obedient to a generalization, corresponds, of course, with no reality, either in the United States or anywhere else; it is the petrifaction of a fear very common in Europe today—a fear of the future. Where, in a more hopeful era, America embodied for Europe a certain millennial promise, now in the Atomic Age it embodies an evil presentiment of a millennium just at hand. To Mlle. de Beauvoir, obsessed with memories of Jules Verne, America is a symbol of a mechanical progress once dreamed of and now repudiated with horror; it is a Judgment on itself and on Europe. No friendly experience with Americans can dispel this deep-lying dread. She does not wish to know America but only to ascertain that it is there, just as she had imagined it. She shrinks from involvement in this "big steel world" and makes no attempt to see factories, workers, or political leaders. She prefers the abstraction of "Wall Street."

This recoil from American actuality has the result that might be expected, a result, in fact, so predictable that one might say she willed it. Her book is consistently misinformed in small matters as well as large. She has a

gift for visual description which she uses very successfully to evoke certain American phenomena: Hollywood,
the Grand Canyon, the Bronx, Chinatown, women's
dresses, the stockyards, the Bowery, Golden Gate, auto
camps, Hawaiian dinners, etc. In so far as the U.S. is a
vast tourist camp, a vacationland, a Stop-in Serv-Urself,
she has caught its essence. But in so far as the United
States is something more than a caricature of itself conceived by the mind of an ad man or a Western Chamber
of Commerce, she has a disinclination to view it. She
cannot, for example, take in the names of American
writers even when she has their books by her elbow: she
speaks repeatedly of James Algee (Agee), of Farrel
(Farrell), O'Neil (O'Neill), and of Max Twain—a
strange form of compliment to authors whom she pro-
fesses to like. In the same way, Greenwich Village, which
she loves, she speaks of throughout as "Greeniwich,"
even when she comes to live there.

These are minor distortions. What is more pathetic
is her credulity, which amounts to a kind of superstition. She is so eager to appear well informed that she
believes anything anybody tells her, especially if it is
anti-American and pretends to reveal the inner work-
ings of the capitalist mechanism. The Fifth Avenue shops,
she tells us, are "reserved for the capitalist international,"
and no investigative instinct tempts her to cross the bar-
ricade and see for herself. Had she done so, she might
have found suburban housewives, file clerks, and stenog-
raphers swarming about the racks of Peck & Peck or
Best's or Franklin Simon's, and colored girls mingling
with white girls at the counters of Saks Fifth Avenue. A
Spanish painter assures her that in America you have
to hire a press agent to get your paintings shown. An
author tells her that in America literary magazines print
only favorable reviews. A student tells her that in America private colleges pay better salaries than state universities, so that the best education falls to the privileged
classes, who do not want it, and so on. At Vassar, she

relates, students are selected "according to their intellectual capacities, family, and fortune." Every item in this catalogue is false. (Private colleges do not pay better salaries—on the contrary, with a few exceptions, they pay notoriously worse; family plays no part in the selection of students at Vassar, and fortune only to the extent that the tuition has to be paid by someone—friend, parent, or scholarship donor; you do not have to hire a press agent; some literary magazines make a positive specialty of printing unfavorable reviews.)

Yet Mlle. de Beauvoir, unsuspecting, continues volubly to pass on "the low-down" to her European readers: there is no friendship between the sexes in America; American whites are "stiff" and "cold"; American society has lost its mobility; capital is in "certain hands," and the worker's task is "carefully laid out." "True, a few accidental successes give the myth of the self-made man a certain support, but they are illusory and tangential . . ."

The picture of an America that consists of a small ruling class and a vast inert, regimented mass beneath it is elaborated at every opportunity. She sees the dispersion of goods on counters but draws no conclusion from it as to the structure of the economy. The American worker, to her, is invariably the French worker, a consecrated symbol of oppression. She talks a great deal of American conformity but fails to recognize a thing that Tocqueville saw long ago; that this conformity is the expression of a predominantly middle-class society; it is the price paid (as yet) for the spread of plenty. Whether the diffusion of television sets is, in itself, a good is another question; the fact is, however, that they *are* diffused; the "Pullman class," for weal or woe, does not have a corner on them, or on the levers of political power.

The outrage of the upper-class minority at the spectacle of television aerials on the shabby houses of Poverty Row, at the thought of the Frigidaires and washing machines in farmhouse and working-class kitchens, at the

new cars parked in ranks outside the factories, at the
very thought of installment buying, unemployment com-
pensation, social security, trade-union benefits, veterans'
housing, at General Vaughan, above all at Truman the
haberdasher, the symbol of this cocky equality—their
outrage is perhaps the most striking phenomenon in
American life today. Yet Mlle. de Beauvoir remained
unaware of it, and unaware also, for all her journal tells
us, of income taxes and inheritance taxes, of the expense
account and how it has affected buying habits and given
a peculiar rashness and transiency to the daily experience
of consumption. It can be argued that certain angry elements in American business do not know their own interests, which lie in the consumers' economy; even so,
this ignorance and anger are an immense political fact in
America.

The society characterized by Mlle. de Beauvoir as
"rigid," "frozen," "closed" is in the process of great
change. The mansions are torn down and the real-estate
"development" takes their place: serried rows of ranch-
type houses, painted in pastel colors, each with its picture
window and its garden, each equipped with deep-
freeze, oil furnace, and automatic washer, spring up in
the wilderness. Class barriers disappear or become
porous; the factory worker is an economic aristocrat in
comparison to the middle-class clerk; even segregation is
diminishing; consumption replaces acquisition as an incentive. The America invoked by Mlle. de Beauvoir as a
country of vast inequalities and dramatic contrasts is
rapidly ceasing to exist.

One can guess that it is the new America, rather than
the imaginary America of economic royalism, that
creates in Mlle. de Beauvoir a feeling of mixed attraction
and repulsion. In one half of her sensibility, she is greatly
excited by the United States and precisely by its material
side. She is fascinated by drugstore displays of soap and
dentifrices, by the uniformly regulated traffic, by the

"good citizenship" of Americans, by the anonymous
camaraderie of the big cities, by jazz and expensive record players and huge collections of records, and above
all—to speak frankly—by the orange juice, the martinis,
and the whiskey. She speaks elatedly of "my" America,
"my" New York; she has a child's greedy possessiveness
toward this place which she is in the act of discovering.

Toward the end of the book, as she revises certain
early judgments, she finds that she has become "an American." What she means is that she has become somewhat
critical of the carnival aspects of American life which
at first bewitched her; she is able to make discriminations
between different kinds of jazz, different hotels, different
night clubs. Very tentatively, she pushes beyond appearance and perceives that the American is not his
possessions, that the American character is not fleshly but
abstract. Yet at bottom she remains disturbed by what she
has seen and felt, even marginally, of the American problem. This is not one of inequity, as she would prefer to believe, but of its opposite. The problem posed by the
United States is, as Tocqueville saw, the problem of
equality, its consequences, and what price shall be paid
for it. How is wealth to be spread without the spread of
uniformity? How create a cushion of plenty without stupefaction of the soul and the senses? It is a dilemma that
glares from every picture window and whistles through
every breezeway.

If Americans, as Mlle. de Beauvoir thinks, are apa-
thetic politically, it is because they can take neither side
with any great conviction—how can one be *against* the
abolition of poverty? And how, on the other hand, can
one champion a leveling of extremes? For Europeans of
egalitarian sympathies, America *is* this dilemma, relent-
lessly marching toward them, a future which "works,"
and which for that very reason they have no wish to
face. Hence the desire, so very evident in Mlle. de
Beauvoir's impressions and in much journalism of the
European left, not to know what America is really like,
to identify it with "fascism" or "reaction," not to admit, in

short, that it has realized, to a considerable extent, the economic and social goals of President Franklin D. Roosevelt and of progressive thought in general.

January, 1952

The American Realist
Playwrights

As soon as this title is announced for a lecture or an article, a question pops up: who are they? Is there, as is assumed abroad, a school of realists in the American theatre or is this notion a critical figment? The question is legitimate and will remain, I hope, in the air long after I have finished. Nevertheless, for purposes of discussion, I am going to take for granted that there is such a group, if not a school, and name its members: Arthur Miller, Tennessee Williams, William Inge, Paddy Chayevsky, the Elmer Rice of *Street Scene*. Behind them, casting them in the shadow, stands the great figure of O'Neill, and opposite them, making them seem more homogeneous, are writers like George Kelly, Wilder, Odets, Saroyan. Their counterparts in the novel are Dreiser, Sherwood Anderson, James T. Farrell, the early Thomas Wolfe—which illustrates, by the way, the backwardness of the theatre in comparison with the novel. The theatre seems to be chronically twenty years behind, regardless of realism, as the relation of Beckett to Joyce, for example, shows. The theatre feeds on the novel; never vice versa: think of the hundreds of dramatizations of novels, and then try to think of a book that was "novelized" from a play. There is not even a word for it. The only actual case I can call to mind is *The Other House* by Henry James—a minor novel he salvaged from a play of his own that failed. To return to the main subject, one characteristic of American realism in the theatre is that none of its practitioners currently—except Chayevsky—wants to call himself a realist. Tennessee Williams is known to his admirers as a "poetic realist," while Arthur Miller declares that he is an exponent of the "social play" and identifies himself with the Greek playwrights, whom he describes as social playwrights also. This delusion was dramatized, if that is the word, in *A View from the Bridge*.

The fact that hardly a one of these playwrights cares to be regarded as a realist without some qualifying or mitigating adjective's being attached to the term invites a definition of realism. What does it mean in common parlance? I have looked the word "realist" up in the Oxford English Dictionary. Here is what they say. ". . . In reference to art and literature, sometimes used as a term of commendation, when precision and vividness of detail are regarded as a merit, and sometimes unfavorably contrasted with idealized description or representation. In recent use it has often been used with the implication that the details are of an unpleasant or sordid character." This strikes me as a very fair account of the historical fate of the notion of realism, but I shall try to particularize a little, in the hope of finding out why and how this happened. And I shall not be condemning realism but only noting what people seem to think it is.

When we say that a novel or a play is realistic, we mean, certainly, that it gives a picture of ordinary life. Its characters will be drawn from the middle class, the lower middle class, occasionally the working class. You cannot write realistic drama about upper-class life; at least, no one ever has. Aristocracy does not lend itself to realistic treatment, but to one or another kind of stylization: romantic drama, romantic comedy, comedy of manners, satire, tragedy. This fact in itself is a realistic criticism of the aristocratic idea, which cannot afford, apparently, to live in the glass house of the realistic stage. Kings and noble men, said Aristotle, are the protagonists of tragedy—not women or slaves. The same is true of nobility of character or intellect. The exceptional man, whether he be Oedipus or King Lear or one of the romantic revolutionary heroes of Hugo or Musset, is fitted to be the protagonist of a tragedy, but just this tragic fitness disqualifies him from taking a leading role in a realist drama. Such figures as Othello or Hernani can never be the subject of realistic treatment, unless it is with the object of deflating them, showing how *ordinary*—petty or squalid—they are. But then the hero is no longer Othello but an impostor posing as Othello. Cut down to size, he is just like everybody else but worse, because he is a fraud into the bargain. This abrupt foreshortening is why realistic treatment of upper-class life always takes the harsh plunge into satire. No man is a hero to his valet, and Beaumarchais' Figaro is the spokesman of social satire—not of realism; his personal and private realism turns his master into a clown. Realism deals with ordinary men and women or, in extreme forms, with sub-ordinary men, men on the level of beasts or of blind conditioned reflexes (*La Bête Humaine, The Hairy Ape*). This tendency is usually identified with naturalism, but I am regarding naturalism as simply a variety of realism.

Realism, historically, is associated with two relatively modern inventions., i.e., with journalism and with photography. "Photographic realism" is a pejorative term, and enemies of realistic literature often dismissed it as "no more than journalism," implying that journalism was a sordid, seamy affair—a daily photographic close-up, as it were, of the clogged pores of society. The author as sheer observer likened himself to a camera (Dos Passos, Christopher Isherwood, Wright Morris), and insofar as the realistic novel was vowed to be a reflector of ordinary life, the newspapers inevitably became a prime source of material. Newspaper accounts impressed the nineteenth century with their quality of "stark objectivity," and newspapers, which appeared every day, seemed to be the repositories of everydayness and to give a multiple image of the little tragedies and vicissitudes of daily life. In America, in the early part of this century, the realistic novel was a partner of what was called "muckraking" journalism, and both were linked with populism and crusades for political reform.

Hence, perhaps, in part, the unsavory associations in common speech of the word "realistic," even when applied in nonliterary contexts. Take the phrase "a realistic decision." If someone tells you he is going to make "a realistic decision," you immediately understand that he has resolved to do something bad. The same with "Realpolitik." A "realistic politics" is a euphemism for a politics of harsh opportunism; if you hear someone say that it is time for a government to follow a realistic line, you can interpret this as meaning that it is time for principles to be abandoned. A politician or a political thinker who calls himself a political realist is usually boasting that he sees politics, so to speak, in the raw; he is generally a proclaimed cynic and pessimist who makes it his business to look behind words and fine speeches for the motive. This motive is always low.

Whatever the field, whenever you hear that a subject is to be treated "realistically," you expect that its unpleasant aspects are to be brought forward. So it is with the play and the novel. A delicate play like Turgenev's *A Month in the Country,* though perfectly truthful to life, seems deficient in realism in comparison with the stronger medicine of Gorki's *The Lower Depths.* This is true of Turgenev's novels as well and of such English writers as Mrs. Gaskell. And of the peaceful parts of *War and Peace.* Ordinary life treated in its uneventful aspects tends to turn into an idyl. We think of Turgenev and Mrs. Gaskell almost as pastoral writers, despite the fact that their faithful sketches have nothing in common with the artificial convention of the true pastoral. We suspect that there is something arcadian here—something "unrealistic."

If realism deals with the ordinary man embedded in ordinary life, which for the most part is uneventful, what then is the criterion that makes us forget Turgenev or Mrs. Gaskell when we name off the realists? I think it is this: what we call realism, and particularly dramatic real-

ism, tends to single out the ordinary man at the moment
he might get into the newspaper. The criterion, in other
words, is drawn from journalism. The ordinary man must
become "news" before he qualifies to be the protagonist
of a realistic play or novel. The exceptional man is news
at all times, but how can the ordinary man get into the
paper? By committing a crime. Or, more rarely, by getting involved in a spectacular accident. Since accidents, in
general, are barred from the drama, this leaves crime—
murder or suicide or embezzlement. And we find that the
protagonists of realistic drama, by and large, are the protagonists of newspaper stories—"little men" who have shot
their wives or killed themselves in the garage or gone to
jail for fraud or embezzlement. Now drama has always
had an affinity for crime; long before realism was known,
Oedipus and Clytemnestra and Macbeth and Othello were
famous for their deeds of blood. But the crimes of tragedy
are the crimes of heroes, while the crimes of realistic
drama are the crimes of the nondescript person, the
crimes that are, in a sense, all alike. The individual in the
realistic drama is regarded as a cog or a statistic; he commits the uniform crime that sociologically he might be expected to commit. That is, supposing that 1,031 bookkeepers in the state of New York are destined to tamper
with the accounts, and 304 policemen are destined to
shoot their wives, and 1,115 householders to do away with
themselves in the garage, each individual bookkeeper, cop,
and householder has been holding a ticket in this statistical lottery, like the fourteen Athenian youths and maidens
sent off yearly to the Minotaur's labyrinth, and he ac-
quires interest for the realist theatre only when his "number" comes up. To put it as simply as possible, the cop in
Street Scene commits his crime—wife-murder—without
having the moral freedom to choose to commit it, just as
Willy Loman in *Death of a Salesman* commits suicide—
under sociological pressure. The hero of tragedy, on the
contrary, is a morally free being who identifies himself
with his crime (i.e., elects it), and this is true even where
he is fated, like Oedipus, to commit it and can be said to

have no personal choice in the matter. Oedipus both rejects and accepts his deeds, embraces them in free will at last as *his*. It is the same with Othello or Hamlet. The distinction will be clear if you ask yourself what tragedy of Shakespeare is closest to the realistic theatre. The answer, surely, is *Macbeth*. And why? Because of Lady Macbeth. Macbeth really doesn't choose to murder the sleeping Duncan; Lady Macbeth chooses for him; he is like a middle-class husband, nagged on by his ambitious wife, the way the second vice-president of a bank is nagged on by his Mrs. Macbeth, who wants him to become first vice-president. The end of the tragedy, however, reverses all this; Macbeth becomes a hero only late in the drama, when he pushes Lady Macbeth aside and takes all his deeds on himself. Paradoxically, the conspicuous tragic hero is never free *not* to do his deed; he cannot escape it, as Hamlet found. But the mute hero or protagonist of a realistic play is always free, at least seemingly, not to emerge from obscurity and get his picture in the paper. There is always the chance that not he but some other nondescript bookkeeper or policeman will answer the statistical call.

The heroes of realistic plays are clerks, bookkeepers, policemen, housewives, salesmen, schoolteachers, small and middling businessmen. They commit crimes but they cannot be professional criminals (unlike the heroes of Gênet or the characters in *The Beggar's Opera*), for professional criminals, like kings and noble men, are a race apart. The settings of realistic plays are offices, drab dining rooms or living rooms, or the backyard, which might be defined as a place where some grass has once been planted and failed to grow. The backyard is a favorite locus for American realist plays, but no realist play takes place in a garden. Nature is excluded from the realist play, as it has been from the realistic novel. The presence of Nature in Turgenev (and in Chekhov) denotes, as I have suggested, a pastoral intrusion. If a realist play does not take place in the backyard, where Nature has been eroded by clothes-poles, garbage cans, bottled-gas tanks, and so on, it takes place indoors, where the only plant, generally, is a rubber plant. Even with Ibsen, the action is confined to a room or pair of rooms until the late plays like *A Lady from the Sea, The Master Builder, John Gabriel Borkman,* when the realistic style has been abandoned for symbolism and the doors are swung open to the garden, mountains, the sea. Ibsen, however, is an exception to the general rule that the indoor scene must be unattractive: his middle-class Scandinavians own some handsome furniture; Nora's house, like any doll's house, must have been charmingly appointed. But Ibsen is an exception to another rule that seems to govern realistic drama (and the novel too, for that matter)—the rule that it must not be well written. (Thanks to William Archer's wooden translations, his work now falls into line in English.) This rule in America has the force, almost, of a law, one of those iron laws that work from within necessity itself, apparently, and without conscious human aid. Our American realists do not *try* to write badly. Many, like Arthur Miller, strive to write "well," i.e., pretentiously, but like Dreiser in the novel they are cursed with inarticulateness. They "grope." They are, as O'Neill said of himself, "fogbound."

The heroes are petty or colorless; the settings are drab; the language is lame. Thus the ugliness of the form is complete. I am not saying this as a criticism, only observing that when a play or a novel fails to meet these norms, we cease to think of it as realistic. Flaubert, known to be a "stylist," ceases to count for us as a realist, and even in the last century, Matthew Arnold, hailing Tolstoy as a realist, was blinded by categorical thinking—with perhaps a little help from the translations—into calling his novels raw "slices of life," sprawling, formless, and so on. But it is these clichés, in the long run, that have won out. The realistic novel today is more like what Arnold thought Tolstoy was than it is like Tolstoy or any of the early realists. This question of the beauty of form also touches the actor. An actor formerly was supposed to be a good-looking man, with a handsome figure, beautiful

movements, and a noble diction. These attributes are no
longer necessary for a stage career; indeed, in America
they are a positive handicap. A good-looking young man
who moves well and speaks well is becoming almost un-
employable in American "legit" theatre; his best hope today is to look for work in musical comedy. Or posing
for advertisements. On the English stage, where realism
until recently never got a foothold, the good-looking actor
still rules the roost, but the English actor cannot play
American realist parts, while the American actor cannot
play Shakespeare or Shaw. A pretty girl in America may
still hope to be an actress, though even here there are
signs of a change: the heroine of O'Neill's late play, *A
Moon for the Misbegotten,* was a freckled giantess five
feet eleven inches tall and weighing 180 pounds.

Eisenstein and the Italian neo-realists used people off
the street for actors—a logical inference from premises
which, being egalitarian and documentary, are essentially
hostile to professional élites, including Cossacks, Swiss
Guards, and actors. The professional actor in his grease-
paint is the antithesis of the pallid man on the street. But
film and stage realism are not so democratic in their principles as may at first appear. To begin with, the director
and a small corps of professionals—electricians and cam-
eramen—assume absolute power over the masses, i.e.,
over the untrained actors picked from the crowd; no resistance is encountered, as it would be with professional
actors, in molding the human material to the director-
dictator's will. And even with stars and all-professional
casts, the same tendency is found in the modern realist or
neo-realist director. Hence the whispered stories of stars
deliberately broken by a director: James Dean and Bri-
gitte Bardot. Similar stories of brainwashing are heard
backstage. This is not surprising if realism, as we now
know it, rejects as nonaverage whatever is noble, beautiful, or seemly, whatever is capable of "gesture," whatever
in fact is free. Everything I have been saying up till now
can be summed up in a sentence. Realism is a depreciation
of the real. It is a gloomy puritan doctrine that has flour-

ished chiefly in puritan countries—America, Ireland, Scandinavia, northern France, nonconformist England—chilly, chilblained countries, where the daily world is ugly and everything is done to keep it so, as if as a punishment for sin. The doctrine is spreading with industrialization, the growth of ugly cities, and the erosion of Nature. It came late to the English stage, long after it had appeared in the novel, because those puritan elements with which it is naturally allied have, up until now, considered the theatre to be wicked.

At the same time, in defense of realism, it must be said that its great enemy has been just that puritan life whose gray color it has taken. The original realists—Ibsen in the theatre, Flaubert in the novel—regarded themselves as "pagans," in opposition to their puritan contemporaries, and adhered to a religion of Beauty or Nature; they dreamed of freedom and hedonistic license (Flaubert) and exalted (Ibsen) the autonomy of the individual will. Much of this "paganism" is still found in O'Casey and in the early O'Neill, a curdled puritan of Irish-American stock. The original realists were half Dionysian aesthetes ("The vine-leaves in his hair") and their heroes and heroines were usually rebels, protesting the drabness and meanness of the common life. Ibsen's characters complain that they are "stifling"; in the airless hypocrisy of the puritan middle-class parlor, people were being poisoned by the dead gas of lies. Hypocrisy is the cardinal sin of the middle class, and the exposure of a lie is at the center of all Ibsen's plots. The strength and passion of realism is its resolve to tell the whole truth; this explains why the realist in his indictment of society avoids the old method of satire with its delighted exaggeration. The realist drama at its highest is an implacable exposé. Ibsen rips off the curtain and shows his audiences to themselves, and there is something inescapable in the manner of the confrontation, like a case slowly being built. The pillars of society who sit in the best seats are, bit by bit, informed that they are rotten and that the commerce they live on is a commerce of "coffin ships." The action on the Ibsen stage is too close for comfort to the lives of the audience; only the invisible "fourth wall" divides them. "This is the way we live now!" Moral examination, self-examination are practical as a duty, a protestant stock-taking, in the realist mission hall.

For this, it is essential that the audience accept the picture as true; it cannot be permitted to feel that it is watching something "made up" or embellished. Hence the stripping down of the form and the elimination of effects that might be recognized as literary. For the first time too, in the realist drama, the accessories of the action are described at length by the playwright. The details must strike home and convince. The audience must be able to place the furniture, the carpets, the ornaments, the napery and glassware as "just what these people would have." This accounts for the importance of the stage set. Many critics who scornfully dismiss the "boxlike set" of the realistic drama, with its careful disposition of furniture, do not understand its function. This box is the box or "coffin" of average middle-class life opened at one end to reveal the corpse within, looking, as all embalmed corpses are said to do, "just as if it were alive." Inside the realist drama, whenever it is genuine and serious, there is a kind of double illusion, a false bottom: everything appears to be lifelike but this appearance of life is death. The stage set remains a central element in all true realism; it cannot be replaced by scrim or platforms. In *A Long Day's Journey into Night,* surely the greatest realist drama since Ibsen, the family living room, with its central overhead lighting-fixture, is as solid and eternal as oak and as sad as wicker, and O'Neill in the text tells the stage-designer what books must be in the glassed-in bookcase on the left and what books in the other by the entrance. The tenement of Elmer Rice's *Street Scene* (in the opera version) was a magnificent piece of characterization; so was the Bronx living room of Odets' *Awake and Sing*—his sole (and successful) experiment with realism. I can still see the bowl of fruit on the table, slightly to the left of stage center, and hear the Jewish mother interrupting whoever

happened to be talking, to say, "Have a piece of fruit."
That bowl of fruit, which *was* the Jewish Bronx, remains
more memorable as a character than many of the people
in the drama. This gift of characterization through props
and stage set is shared by Paddy Chayevsky in *Middle of
the Night* and by William Inge in *Come Back, Little Sheba,*
where an unseen prop or accessory, the housewife's terrible frowsty little dog, is a master-stroke of realist illusion-
ism and, more than that, a kind of ghostly totem. All these
plays, incidentally, are stories of death-in-life.

This urgent correspondence with a familiar reality,
down to the last circumstantial detail, is what makes realism so gripping, like a trial in court. The dramatist is witnessing or testifying, on an oath never sworn before in a
work of art, not to leave out anything and to tell the
truth to the best of his ability. And yet the realistic dramatist, beginning with Ibsen, is aware of a missing element.
The realist mode seems to generate a dissatisfaction with
itself, even in the greatest masters: Tolstoy, for example,
came to feel that his novels, up to *Resurrection,* were in-
consequential trifling; the vital truth had been left out. In
short, as a novelist, he began to feel like a hypocrite. This
dissatisfaction with realism was evidently suffered also by
Ibsen; halfway through his realist period, you see him
start to look for another dimension. Hardly had he discovered or invented the new dramatic mode than he
showed signs of being cramped by it; he experienced, if
his plays are an index, that same sense of confinement, of
being stifled, within the walls of realism that his characters
experience within the walls of middle-class life. Something
was missing: air. This is already plain in *The Wild Duck,*
a strange piece of auto-criticism and probably his finest
play; chafing, restless, mordant, he is searching for something else, for a poetic element, which he represents, finally, in the wild duck itself, a dramatic symbol for that cherished wild freedom that neither Ibsen nor his characters
can maintain, without harming it, in a shut-in space. But
to resort to symbols to make good the missing element
becomes a kind of forcing, like trying to raise a wild bird

in an attic, and the strain of this is felt in *Rosmersholm,* where symbols play a larger part and are charged with a more oppressive weight of meaning. In *The Lady from the Sea, The Master Builder,* and other late plays, the symbols have broken through the thin fence or framework of realism; poetry has spread its crippled wings, but the price has been heavy.

The whole history of dramatic realism is encapsulated in Ibsen. First, the renunciation of verse and of historical and philosophical subjects in the interests of prose and the present time; then the dissatisfaction and the attempt to restore the lost element through a recourse to symbols; then, or at the same time, a forcing of the action at the climaxes to heighten the drama; finally, the renunciation of realism in favor of a mixed mode or hodgepodge. The reaching for tragedy at the climaxes is evident in *Hedda Gabler* and still more so in *Rosmersholm,* where, to me at any rate, the climactic shriek "To the mill race!" is absurdly like a bad film. Many of Ibsen's big moments, even as early as *A Doll's House,* strike me as false and grandiose, that is, precisely, as stagey. Nor is it only in the context of realism that they appear so. It is not just that one objects that people do not act or talk like that —Tolstoy's criticism of King Lear on the heath. If you compare the mill-race scene in *Rosmersholm* with the climax of a Shakespearean tragedy, you will see that the Shakespearean heroes are far less histrionic, more natural and *ordinary;* there is always a stillness at the center of the Shakespearean storm. It is as if the realist, in reaching for tragedy, were punished for his *hubris* by a ludicrous fall into bathos. Tragedy is impossible by definition in the quotidian realist mode, since (quite aside from the question of the hero) tragedy is the exceptional action one of whose signs is beauty.

In America the desire to supply the missing element (usually identified as poetry or "beauty") seems to grow stronger and stronger exactly in proportion to the author's awkwardness with language. The less a playwright can write prose, the more he wishes to write poetry and to raise his plays by their bootstraps to a higher realm. You find these applications of "beauty" in Arthur Miller and Tennessee Williams; they stand out like rouge on a pitted complexion; it is as though the author first wrote the play naturalistically and then gave it a beauty-treatment or face-lift. Before them, O'Neill, who was too honest and too philosophically inclined to be satisfied by a surface solution, kept looking methodically for a way of representing the missing element in dramas that would still be realistic at the core. He experimented with masks (*The Great God Brown*), with the aside and the soliloquy (*Strange Interlude*), with a story and pattern borrowed from Greek classic drama (*Mourning Becomes Electra*). In other words, he imported into the American home or farm the machinery of tragedy. But his purpose was always a greater realism. His use of the aside, for example, was very different from the traditional use of the aside (a kind of nudge to the audience, usually on the part of the villain, to let them in on his true intent or motive); in *Strange Interlude* O'Neill was trying, through the aside, to make available to the realistic drama the discoveries of modern psychology, to represent on the stage the unconscious selves of his characters, at cross-purposes with their conscious selves but just as real if not realer, at least according to the psychoanalysts. He was trying, in short, to give a more complete picture of ordinary people in their daily lives. It was the same with his use of masks in *The Great God Brown;* he was appropriating the mask of Athenian drama, a ritual means of putting a distance between the human actor and the audience, to bring his own audience closer to the inner humanity of his character—the man behind the mask of conformity. The fact that these devices were clumsy is beside the point. O'Neill's sincerity usually involved him in clumsiness. In the end, he came back to the straight realism of his beginnings: *The Long Voyage Home,* the title of his young Caribbean series, could also be the title of the great play of his old age: *A Long Day's Journey into Night.* He has sailed beyond the horizon and back into port; the circle is complete. In this late play, the quest for the missing element, as such, is renounced; poetry is held to be finally unattainable by the author. "I couldn't touch what I tried to tell you just now," says the character who is supposed to be the young O'Neill. "I just stammered. That's the best I'll ever do. I mean, if I live. Well, it will be faithful realism, at least. Stammering is the native eloquence of us fog people." In this brave acknowledgment or advance acceptance of failure, there is something very moving. Moreover, the acceptance of defeat was in fact the signal of a victory. *A Long Day's Journey into Night,* sheer dogged prose from beginning to end, achieves in fact a peculiar poetry, and the relentless amassing of particulars takes on, eventually, some of the crushing force of inexorable logic that we find in Racine or in a Greek play. The weight of circumstance itself becomes a fate of nemesis. This is the closest, probably, that realism can get to tragedy.

The "stammering" of O'Neill was what made his later plays so long, and the stammering, which irritated some audiences, impatient for the next syllable to fall, was a sign of the author's agonized determination to be truthful. If O'Neill succeeded, at last, in deepening the character of his realism, it was because the missing element he strove to represent was not, in the end, "poetry" or "beauty" or "philosophy" (though he sometimes seems to have felt that it was) but simply meaning—the total significance of an action. What he came to conclude, rather wearily, in his last plays was that the total significance of an action lay in the accumulated minutiae of that action and could not be abstracted from it, at least not by him. There was no truth or meaning beyond the event itself; anything more (or less) would be a lie. This pun or tautology, this conundrum, committed him to a cycle of repetition, and memory, the mother of the Muses, became his only muse.

The younger American playwrights—Miller, Williams, Inge, Chayevsky—now all middle-aged, are pledged, like O'Neill, to verisimilitude. They purport to offer a "slice of life," in Tennessee Williams' case a rich, spicy slab of Southern fruitcake, but still a slice of life. The locus of their plays is the American porch or backyard or living room or parlor or bus station, presented as typical, authentic as home-fried potatoes or "real Vermont maple syrup." This authenticity may be regional, as with Williams and Paddy Chayevsky (the Jewish upper West side; a Brooklyn synagogue) or it may claim to be as broad as the nation, as with Arthur Miller, or somewhere rather central, in between the two, as with William Inge. But in any case, the promise of these playwrights is to show an ordinary home, an ordinary group of bus passengers, a typical manufacturer, and so on, and the dramatis personae tend to resemble a small-town, non-blue-ribbon jury: housewife, lawyer, salesman, chiropractor, workingman, schoolteacher. . . . Though Tennessee Williams' characters are more exotic, they too are offered as samples to the audience's somewhat voyeuristic eye; when Williams' film, *Baby Doll,* was attacked by Cardinal Spellman, the director (Elia Kazan) defended it on the grounds that it was true to life that he and Williams had observed, on location, in Mississippi. If the people in Tennessee Williams were regarded as products of the author's imagination, his plays would lose all their interest. There is always a point in any one of Williams' dramas where recognition gives way to a feeling of shocked incredulity; this shock technique is the source of his sensational popularity. But the audience would not be electrified if it had not been persuaded earlier that it was witnessing something the author vouched for as a common, ordinary occurrence in the Deep South.

Unlike the other playwrights, who make a journalistic claim to neutral recording, Arthur Miller admittedly has a message. His first-produced play, *All My Sons,* was a social indictment taken, almost directly, from Ibsen's *Pillars of Society.* The coffin ships, rotten, unseaworthy vessels caulked over to give an appearance of soundness, become defective airplanes sold to the government by a corner-cutting manufacturer during the Second World War;

like the coffin ships, the airplanes are a symbol of the inner rottenness of bourgeois society, and the sins of the father, as *almost* in Ibsen, are visited on the son, a pilot who cracks up in the Pacific theatre (in Ibsen, the ship-owner's boy is saved at the last minute from sailing on *The Indian Girl*). The insistence on this symbol and the vagueness or absence of concrete detail express Miller's impatience with the particular and his feeling that his play ought to say "more" than it appears to be saying. Ibsen, even in his later, symbolic works, was always specific about the where, when, and how of his histories (the biographies of his central characters are related with almost too much circumstantiality), but Miller has always regarded the specific as trivial and has sought, from the very outset, a hollow, reverberant universality. The reluctance to awaken a specific recognition, for fear that a larger meaning might go unrecognized by the public, grew on Miller with *Death of a Salesman*—a strong and original conception that was enfeebled by its creator's insistence on universality and by a too-hortatory excitement, i.e., an eagerness to preach, which is really another form of the same thing. Miller was bent on making his Salesman (as he calls him) a parable of Everyman, exactly as in a clergyman's sermon, so that the drama has only the quality—and something of the canting tone—of an illustrative moral example. The thirst for universality becomes even more imperious in *A View from the Bridge*, where the account of a waterfront killing that Miller read in a newspaper is accessorized with Greek architecture, "archetypes," and, from time to time, intoned passages of verse, and Miller announces in a preface that he is not interested in his hero's "psychology." Miller does not understand that you cannot turn a newspaper item about Italian longshoremen and illegal immigration into a Greek play by adding a chorus and the pediment of a temple. Throughout Miller's long practice as a realist, there is not only a naïve searching for another dimension but an evident hatred of and contempt for reality—as not good enough to make plays out of.

It is natural, therefore, that he should never have any interest in how people talk; his characters all talk the same way—somewhat funereally, through their noses. A live sense of speech differences (think of Shaw's *Pygmalion*) is rare in American playwrights; O'Neill tried to cultivate it ("dat ol davil sea"), but he could never do more than write perfunctory dialect, rather like that of somebody telling a Pat and Mike story or a mountaineer joke. The only American realist with an ear for speech, aside from Chayevsky, whose range is narrow, is Tennessee Williams. He does really hear his characters, especially his female characters; he has studied their speech patterns and, like Professor Higgins, he can tell where they come from; Williams too is the only realist who places his characters in social history. Of all the realists, after O'Neill, he has probably the greatest native gift for the theatre; he is a natural performer and comedian, and it is too bad that he suffers from the inferiority complex that is the curse of the recent American realists—the sense that a play must be bigger than its characters. This is really a social disease—a fear of being underrated—rather than the claustrophobia of the medium itself, which tormented Ibsen and O'Neill. But it goes back to the same source: the depreciation of the real. Real speech, for example, is not good enough for Williams and from time to time he silences his characters to put on a phonograph record of his special poetic longplay prose.

All dramatic realism is somewhat sadistic; an audience is persuaded to watch something that makes it uncomfortable and from which no relief is offered—no laughter, no tears, no purgation. This sadism had a moral justification, so long as there was the question of the exposure of a lie. But Williams is fascinated by the refinements of cruelty, which with him becomes a form of aestheticism, and his plays, far from baring a lie that society is trying to cover up, titillate society like a peepshow. The curtain is ripped off, to disclose, not a drab scene of ordinary life, but a sadistic exhibition of the kind certain rather specialized tourists pay to see in big cities like New Orleans. With Williams, it is always a case of watching some mangy cat on a hot tin roof. The ungratified sexual organ of an old maid, a young wife married to a homosexual, a subnormal poor white farmer is proffered to the audience as a curiosity. The withholding of sexual gratification from a creature or "critter" in heat for three long acts is Williams' central device; other forms of torture to which these poor critters are subjected are hysterectomy and castration. Nobody, not even the SPCA, would argue that it was a good thing to show the prolonged torture of a dumb animal on the stage, even though the torture were only simulated and animals, in the end, would profit from such cases being brought to light. Yet this, on a human level, is Tennessee Williams' realism—a cat, to repeat, on a hot tin roof. And, in a milder version, it is found again in William Inge's *Picnic*. No one could have prophesied, a hundred years ago, that the moral doctrine of realism would narrow to the point of becoming pornography, yet something like that seems to be happening with such realistic novels as *Peyton Place* and the later John O'Hara and with one branch of the realist theatre. Realism seems to be a highly unstable mode, attracted on the one hand to the higher, on the other to the lower elements in the human scale, tending always to proceed toward its opposite, that is, to irreality, tracing a vicious circle from which it can escape only by repudiating itself. Realism, in short, is forever begging the question—the question of reality. To find the ideal realist, you would first have to find reality. And if no dramatist today, except O'Neill, can accept being a realist in its full implications, this is perhaps because of lack of courage. Ibsen and O'Neill, with all their dissatisfaction, produce major works in the full realist vein; the recent realists get discouraged after a single effort. *Street Scene; All My Sons; The Glass Menagerie; Come Back, Little Sheba; Middle of the Night*, perhaps *Awake and Sing* are the only convincing evidence that exists of an American realist school—not counting O'Neill. If I add *Death of a Sales-man* and *A Streetcar Named Desire*, it is only because I do not know where else to put them.

July, 1961

The Vassar Girl

Like Athena, goddess of wisdom, Vassar College sprang in full battle dress from the head of a man. Incorporated at Poughkeepsie, New York, in 1861, the year of Lincoln's inauguration and the emancipation of the serfs in Russia, it was the first woman's college to be conceived as an idea, a manifesto, a declaration of rights, and a proclamation of equality.

It did not evolve, like Mount Holyoke, chartered in 1836, from a female seminary into a college; it came into being at one stroke, so to speak, equipped with a museum of natural history, a library, a main building modeled on the Tuileries, an observatory with a gigantic telescope, a collection of paintings and a course of study. This was to embrace, in the specifications of the Founder, "the English language and its Literature; other Modern Languages, the Ancient Classics, so far as may be demanded by the spirit of the times; the Mathematics, to such an extent as may be deemed advisable; all the branches of Natural Science . . . Anatomy, Physiology, and Hygiene . . . the elements of Political Economy; some knowledge of Federal and State Constitutions and Laws; Moral Science, particularly as bearing on the filial, conjugal, and parental relations; Aesthetics . . . Domestic Economy . . . last, and most important of all, the daily, systematic Reading and Study of the Holy Scriptures, as the only and all-sufficient Rule of Christian faith and practice...."

The promulgator of this curriculum, which, except for the last proviso, remains the basis of the Vassar education, was not a gentleman of parts or a social reformer, but a self-educated Poughkeepsie brewer, the keeper of an ale and oyster house. Matthew Vassar's farming parents had migrated from England to Dutchess County, New York, when the boy was four years old. He left school at the age of ten to go to work for a neighboring farmer, carrying his few small belongings tied up in a cotton handkerchief. Persistence and hard work had their storied rewards: at forty, he was a successful Poughkeepsie businessman with a good-sized brewery on the river, membership in the Baptist church, an urge toward foreign travel, and strong philanthropic inclinations. Having no children, he determined to attach his name to some lasting benevolent enterprise and settled on woman's education after cautious shopping and advice-seeking. Once, however, he had been fixed in the notion, his plan became clothed in rhetoric and in philosophic axioms: "Woman, having received from her Creator the same intellectual constitution as man, has the same right as man to intellectual culture and development. . . . The mothers of a country mold the character of its citizens, determine its institutions, and shape its destiny. Next to the influence of the mother is that of the female teacher. . . ." His maiden speech to the Board of Trustees at the initial meeting in February, 1861, had the resonance of a sovereign pronouncement: "I have come to the conclusion, that the establishment and endowment of a College for the education of young women is a work which will satisfy my highest aspirations, and will be, under God, a rich blessing to this city and State, to our country and the world."

The authoritative tone is characteristic; it is as though, speaking through the mouth of the elderly, didactic brewer, were the first, fresh Vassar girl. The stiff, exact provisions evoke the basic architecture of the Vassar

campus, different from the colonial republicanism of the
early men's colleges and from the collegiate Gothic of the
late big philanthropy—something purposive and utilitar-
ian: dark-red brick, plainly set-out buildings in the pre-
vailing factory style of the late nineteenth century. In the
phraseology also, candidly revealed, is the first note of
Vassar emulation, of the passion for public service cou-
pled with a yearning for the limelight, a wish to play a
part in the theatre of world events, to perform some
splendid action that will cut one's name in history like a
figure eight in ice.

The essence of Vassar is mythic. Today, despite much
competition, it still figures in the public mind as the
archetypal woman's college. Less intellectual than Rad-
cliffe or Bryn Mawr, less social and weekendish than
Smith, less athletic than Wellesley, less Bohemian than
Bennington, it is nevertheless the stock butt of musical-
comedy jokes and night-club wheezes. It has called down
thunder from the pulpit, provided heroines for popular
ballads; even a girdle bears its name. Like Harvard, it is
always good for a knowledgeable smile from members of
the population who have scarcely heard the name of another college. It signifies a certain *je ne sais quoi;* a whiff
of luxury and the ineffable; plain thinking and high living. If a somehow know-it-all manner is typical of the
Vassar student, the public has a way of winking that it
knows all about Vassar, though this sly wink only inti-
mates that there is something to know. For different people, in fact, at different periods, Vassar can stand for
whatever is felt to be wrong with the modern female:
humanism, atheism, Communism, short skirts, cigarettes,
psychiatry, votes for women, free love, intellectualism. Pre-
eminently among American college women, the Vassar
girl is thought of as carrying a banner. The inscription
on it varies with the era or with the ideas of the beholder
and in the final sense does not matter—the flushed cheek
and tensed arm are what count.

I myself was an ardent literary little girl in an Episco-
pal boarding school on the West Coast, getting up at four

in the morning to write a seventeen-page medieval romance before breakfast, smoking on the fire-escape and thinking of suicide, meeting a crippled boy in the woods by the cindery athletic field, composing a novelette in study hall about the life of a middle-aged prostitute ("Her eyes were turbid as dishwater") when the name, *Vassar,* entered my consciousness through the person of an English teacher. She symbolized to me the critical spirit, wit, cool learning, detachment—everything I suddenly wished to have and to be, from the moment I first heard her light, precise, cutting voice score some pretension, slatternly phrase or construction on the part of her pupils. With blond buns over her ears, gold-rimmed glasses and a teacher's taste in dress, Miss A—— was severe and formidable, yet she smoked, as I knew, on the side, read *The American Mercury* and was shocked by nothing. She advised me to send my novelette to H. L. Mencken for criticism. The idea of going to Vassar and becoming like Miss A—— immediately dominated my imagination. I gave up a snap course in domestic science and registered for Latin. I tutored in Caesar during the summer and coaxed my family. To go east to college was quite a step in Seattle.

What Vassar represented at that time to the uninitiated person can be gathered from the attitude of my Catholic grandmother in Minneapolis, whom I stopped to visit on my way east to Poughkeepsie. She sent for the parish priest to armor me against the "heresy" I should be exposed to. The priest was as embarrassed as I was at the task set him. He contented himself with a few rumbling remarks about the efficacy of prayer and the sacraments, and then admonished the old lady that at Vassar I would find the very best of Western thought, contemporary and classical—I ought to be proud to be going there. Listening breathlessly, I hardly knew whether to be more thrilled by the priest's liberal commendation or by my grandmother's conservative disapproval.

For the majority, perhaps, of the freshmen swarming through Taylor Gate that year for their first interview with the dean, Vassar had some such overtones. Its high, iron-runged, Gothic gate, which swung open on this day to receive the stream of cars laden with luggage, tennis rackets, phonographs, lamps, and musical instruments, was for most of us outlanders, still in our neat cloche hats and careful little traveling suits, a threshold to possibility. (It was the autumn, though we could not foresee it, of the Wall Street crash.) Bucolically set in rolling orchard country just outside the town of Poughkeepsie, with the prospect of long walks and rides along curving back roads and cold red apples to bite; framed by two mirror-like lakes, by a lively off-campus street full of dress shops, antique stores, inns, which were brimming now with parents, brothers, and fiancés, Vassar, still warm and summery, gave the impression of a cornucopia overflowing with promises. The bareheaded Yale boys in roadsters parked outside Taylor Gate; the tall, dazzling girls, upperclassmen, in pale sweaters and skirts, impeccable, with pearls at the throat and stately walks, like goddesses; the vaulted library; the catalogue already marked and starred for courses like Psychology and Philosophy ("The Meaning of Morals, Beauty, Truth, God—open to freshmen by special permission"); the trolley tracks running past the spiked fence downtown to further shopping, adventure, the railroad station, New York, plays, concerts, night clubs, Fifth Avenue bus rides—all this seemed to foretell four years of a Renaissance lavishness, in an academy that was a Forest of Arden and a Fifth Avenue department store combined.

The dean, in her opening address, told us that we were the smallest class ever to be admitted (in recent years, I presume) and hence the most highly selected. She spoke to us of the responsibilities that thereby devolved on us, but to this part I hardly listened, being so filled with the pride and glory of belonging to the very best class in the very best college in America. This feeling did not really leave me during four years in college; Vassar has a peculiar power of conveying a sense of excellence.

After October, 1929, some of us had smaller allowances; my roommate and I no longer went off-campus every night for a dinner beginning with *canapé* of anchovies and going on to artichokes and mushrooms under glass. More of us were on scholarships or using some form of self-help. Typing papers for others, waking friends in the morning, for the first time became regular industries. Some students' fathers were rumored to have shot themselves or to have had nervous breakdowns, but the off-campus shops still prospered, selling grape lemonade, bacon-and-tomato sandwiches, and later 3.2 beer. New York department stores brought dress exhibitions once or twice a year to the tearooms; we bought more than we could afford and charged it. Yale boys came down weekly for the Saturday-night "J" dance, at which the girls were stags and cut in on them. At these times the more prosperous went out to eat at roadhouses, tearooms, or inns in twos, fours, sixes, or eights. The boys carried whiskey in flasks, and sometimes there were gin picnics. One of my friends had an airplane; another girl kept a pet goat, very white and pretty; in the spring of senior year, when cars were permitted, a few roadsters appeared. In New York, we went to plays, musicals, and speakeasies, two or three girls together on a Saturday day leave; on weekends, alone with our beaux. Many of us were engaged.

During our junior year, the word "Communist" first assumed an active reality: a plain girl who was a science major openly admitted to being one. But most of our radicals were Socialists, and throughout that election year they campaigned for Norman Thomas, holding parades and rallies, though in most cases they were too young to vote. We of the "aesthetic" camp considered them jejune and naïve; we were more impressed when we heard, after a poll, that a plurality (as I recall) of the faculty were voting for Thomas that year.

The inert mass of the student body was, as usual, Republican; we aesthetes did not believe in politics, but slightly favored the Democrats. Then our trustee, Franklin Roosevelt, was elected President. Miss Newcomer of

the Economics Department went off to serve on a committee at Albany. Doctor MacCracken, our president, had
lunch with Roosevelt off a tray in the White House—and
we undergraduates felt more than ever that Vassar was
at the center of everything.

With the impetus of the New Deal and memories of
the breadlines behind us, even we aesthetes began reading about Sacco and Vanzetti and Mooney. We wrote
papers for Contemporary Prose Fiction on Dos Passos.
The pretty blue-eyed Republican girls looked troubled
when you talked to them about these things; *their* favorite
book was *Of Human Bondage,* which we despised. The
Socialists made friends with us, though they swore by
Miss Lockwood's press course, and we by Miss Sandison's Renaissance or by Miss Rindge's art or by a course
in Old English or in verse writing: our group, being
aesthetes, was naturally more individualistic. But by the
end of our senior year the Socialists, the aesthetes, and
the pretty Republican girls had been drawn closer together.

We all drank 3.2 beer at night in Mrs. Cary's tearoom,
discussed term papers and politics, sang songs of fare-
well to each other in half-mocking, half-tender accents.
We were happy to be together, our differences of origin
and opinion reconciled in the fresh May darkness, but our
happiness rested on the sense that all this was provisional
and transitory. "Lost now in the wide, wide world," we
sang fervently, but actually almost all of us were joyous
to be leaving college, precisely because we had loved it,
for Vassar had inspired us with the notion that the
wide, wide world was our oyster.

A few years later, a census was taken, and it was discovered that the average Vassar graduate had two-plus
children and was married to a Republican lawyer.

This finding took by surprise even that section of the
alumnae—Vassar Club activists, organizers of benefits
and fund-raising drives—who looked upon it as providential. Here, at last, they felt, was something concrete

to offset newspaper stories of students picketing during a strike in nearby Beacon, students besieging the state legislature in Albany, that would put an end to the rumors of immorality, faddishness, and Bohemianism that, because of a few undergraduates, had clung to the college's public persona for two decades or more. What these figures proved, the alumnae apologists were really implying, was that the Vassar education had not "taken" or had taken only on a small group who were not at all typical of Vassar and who by their un-Vassarish behavior were getting the college a bad name. And yet the statistical Average herself would have been the first to protest (with that touch of apology so characteristic of Vassar women who have not "done" anything later on) that she was not at all representative of Vassar standards and point to some more unconventional classmate as the real Vassar thing.

A wistful respect for the unorthodox is ingrained in the Vassar mentality. The Vassar freshman still comes through Taylor Gate as I did, with the hope of being made over, redirected, vivified. The daughter of a conservative lawyer, doctor, banker, or businessman, she will have chosen Vassar in all probability with the idea of transcending her background. And if she does not have such plans for herself, her teachers have them for her. If she is, say, a Vassar daughter or a girl from a preparatory school like Chapin or Madeira who chose Vassar because her friends did, her teachers, starting freshman year, will seek to "shake her up," "emancipate" her, make her "think for herself." This dynamic conception of education is Vassar's hallmark.

The progressive colleges have something similar, but there the tendency is to orient the student in some preconceived direction—toward the modern dance or toward "progressive" political thinking, while at Vassar, by and large, the student is almost forbidden to take her direction from the teacher. "What do *you* think?" is the question that ricochets on the student if she asks the teacher's opinion; and the difference between Vassar and the traditional liberal college (where the teacher is also supposed to keep his own ideas in the background) is that at Vassar the student is obliged, every day, to proffer hers.

Thus at a freshman English class I recently visited, the students were discussing Richard Hughes' *The Innocent Voyage,* a book whose thesis is that children are monsters, without moral feeling in the adult sense, insane, irresponsible, incapable of conventional grief or remorse. This idea was very shocking to perhaps half the class, well-brought-up little girls who protested that children were not "like that," indignant hands waved in the air, anguished faces grimaced, while a more detached student in braids testified that her own experience as a babysitter bore Mr. Hughes out. The teacher took no sides but merely smiled and encouraged one side and then the other, raising a hand for quiet when the whole class began shouting at once, and interrupting only to ask, "Do you really know children? Are you speaking from what you have seen or remember, or from what you think *ought* to be so?" This book plainly was chosen not because it was a favorite with the professor or even because of its literary merits but because it challenged preconceptions and disturbed set ideas.

The effect of this training is to make the Vassar student, by the time she has reached her junior year, look back upon her freshman self with pity and amazement. When you talk to her about her life in college, you will find that she sees it as a series of before-and-after snapshots: "When I came to Vassar, I thought like Mother and Daddy . . . I was conservative in my politics . . . I had race prejudice . . . I liked academic painting." With few exceptions, among those who are articulate and who feel that the college has "done something" for them, the trend is from the conservative to the liberal, from the orthodox to the heterodox, with stress on the opportunities Vassar has provided for getting to know "different" people, of opposite opinions and from different backgrounds.

Yet the statistical fate of the Vassar girl, thanks to Mother and Dad and the charge account, is already decreed. And the result is that the Vassar alumna, uniquely among American college women, is two persons—the housewife or matron, and the yearner and regretter. The Vassar graduate who has failed to make a name for herself, to "keep up," extend her interests, is, because of her training, more poignantly conscious of backsliding than her contemporary at Barnard or Holyoke. And unlike the progressive-college graduate, on the other hand, who has been catered to and conciliated by her instructors, the Vassar girl who drifts into matronhood or office work is more inclined to blame herself than society for what has happened, and to feel that she has let the college down by not becoming famous or "interesting." The alumnae records are full of housewives, doctors, teachers, educators, social workers, childwelfare specialists, public-health consultants. But the Vassar dream obdurately prefers such figures as Inez Milholland, '09, who rode a white horse down Fifth Avenue campaigning for woman suffrage; Edna St. Vincent Millay, '17, the *révoltée* girl-poet who made herself a byword of sexual love and disenchanted lyricism; Elizabeth Hawes, '25, iconoclastic dress designer, and author of *Fashion Is Spinach*. The Vassar romanticism will pass over a college president in favor of an author or journalist—Constance Rourke, '07, pioneer folklorist and author of *American Humor;* Muriel Rukeyser, ex-'34, Eleanor Clark, Elizabeth Bishop, '34, poets and writers, Jean Poletti, '25, Lois ("Lipstick" of *The New Yorker*) Long, '22, Beatrice Berle, '23, noted for her opinions on marriage and for the twin bathtubs she and her husband, Adolf A. Berle, Jr., shared in their Washington house—and it will recognize as its own even such antipodal curiosities as Elizabeth Bentley, '30, the ex-Communist spy queen, and Major Julia Hamblet, '37, the first woman to enlist in the Marines.

The incongruities on this list are suggestive. An *arresting performance* in politics, fashion, or art is often taken by the Vassar mind to be synonymous with true accomplishment. The Vassar dynamism drives toward money and success and the limelight in a truly Roman fashion, when it is not yoked to their opposite—service. With its alertness, its eagerness to *do* things, it tends, once the academic restraints are removed, to succumb to a rather journalistic notion of what constitutes value.

In the arts, after the first few intransigent gestures, Vassar talent streams into commercial side lines—advertising, fashion writing, publicity, promotion—and here assurance and energy case the Vassar success woman in an elephant-hide of certainties—a sort of proud flesh. This older Vassar career woman is nearly as familiar to American folklore as the intrepid young Portia or Rosalind she may at one time have passed for. Conscious of being set apart by a superior education, confident of her powers in her own field of enterprise, she is impervious to the universe, which she dominates, both mentally and materially. On the campus, she is found at vocational conferences, panel discussions, committee meetings—she is one of those women who are always dominating, in an advisory capacity. In the world, she is met in political-action groups, consumers' leagues, on school boards and in charitable drives, at forums and round-tables. Married, almost professionally so, the mother of children, she is regarded as a force in her community or business, is respected and not always liked. Vassar, of course, has no patent on this model of the American woman, but there is a challenge in the Vassar atmosphere that makes her graduates feel that they owe it as a positive duty to the college and to the human community to be outstanding, aggressive, and secure.

All this is still far away from the current undergraduate. She has heard vaguely through the alumnae magazine that some Vassar graduates are unhappy and frustrated because college did not prepare them for a life of dishwashing and babies, but this prospect for herself appears to have no relevance, though she may be planning to marry immediately on graduation and to begin

having children at once. The Vassar career woman
she is aware of, without self-identification. Vassar girls
today, even more than most young people, seem to live in
an ideal present; the alumnae they are heading to become
seem as remote to them as the freshman selves they have
transcended. They knit, play bridge, attend classes and
lectures, looking decorous and polite, with smooth, soft
coiffures and tranquil faces. Their plans are made—one
will be a doctor; one will work for the UN; another will
take up journalism. There is none of the conflict and in-
decision that harried us in the thirties; they have decided
to help the world, but not to change or destroy it. They
prepare their work with competence, recite with poise
and credit; in mastery of assigned material, some of it
quite difficult, they outdo any group of college students I
have had experience with. In the classroom, a serene
low voice begs elucidation of a point in a Platonic dialogue: "I'm not sure I understand what Socrates means to
say here." The difficulty is explained— "Thank you," and
a note is taken. Among the upperclassmen, these nods of
illumination and swift scribbles on the note pad are fre-
quent; the college is businesslike.

They read Sartre and Tennessee Williams as part of
their work in the drama; a class in Aesthetics is popular;
they listen to music in the dormitories; but, despite competence, civility, and even deferential interest, they have
an air of placid aloofness from what is currently going
on in the world of arts and letters. All that appears distant
to them; they ask about the names of current authors in
the same tone of dreamy, faraway curiosity as they ask
about the Vassar of fifteen or twenty years ago. Has the
college changed much, they inquire, certain that it has
changed immeasurably because *they* are there. The so-
called literary renaissance of Vassar during the thirties
is something they now hear of with amazement and for
the very first time. Reversing the situation in most colleges, the faculty is ahead of the student body in its
awareness of the times. To the student, the immediate
Vassar is the planet.

If you ask a Vassar undergraduate today to define what a Vassar girl essentially is, she will repulse the thought of a Vassar *stereotype*, as she calls it, and tell you that Vassar is a collection of very different "individuals." Yet this reply, to the ears of an alumna, is a highly Vassar remark, indicating a certain virtuous superiority of popular error.

In many ways, Vassar *has* changed. The campus remains the same—the two lakes; the walk through the pines; Sunset Hill; the deserted golf course; the six spare buildings of the Quadrangle; the Main Hall with its porte-cochere, busy Message Center and post office, dark parlors, and bright bulletin boards; the old riding academy housing the theatre and the classics department; the old observatory; the hemlocks; the new gymnasium; the bulging fieldstone Gothic of the Euthenics Building; the Circle with its brilliant rim of spring flowers, where class picnics are held; the two suburbanish faculty dormitories; the Shakespeare Garden; the outdoor theatre, a great green stadium overlooking the lake; the Students' Building, scene of lectures and dances; Taylor Gate. Poughkeepsie and the railroad station by the Hudson are reached by bus along the track where the old trolley once ran, but the burgher town, with its twisting streets, melancholy river light, somber Hudson Valley mansions and tinny store façades, is still held at a distance. Some of the students, as always, do welfare work in the various Community Centers; Luckey-Platt, the serviceable family-style department store, still offers charge accounts to students; Poughkeepsie citizens attend Vassar lectures and plays, and Poughkeepsie matrons hold luncheon parties in the dining room of Alumnae House; but the off-campus life, in the main, centers about a street or two in Arlington, the outlying section in which the campus is located. And this itself is less lively than formerly; a Peck & Peck, a drugstore, an eating place or two, and the Vassar Bank are the principal remains of a once-spirited commercial area, where teashops, inns, and dress shops once flourished on Vassar extravagance.

Today, "off-campus" for the students is mainly represented by Alumnae House, a tall stucco and brown-beamed building that stands on a hill overlooking the college and that plays, significantly, more and more of a part in campus life and politics. Where, in my day, the roadster, the trolley car, and the taxi bore us off the campus and away from the supervisory eye—downtown in groups to a speakeasy, or off with our dates to a roadhouse or a picturesque old inn—today's undergraduates flock up the hill to Alumnae House for beer, Cokes, hamburgers, and Vassar devils (a sort of fudgy cake sundae) in the Pub on week nights; and on weekends, they join their young men in the big lounge-living room for a cocktail or two, under the watchful eyes of the alumnae secretary or her assistants, who see that the young men do not get too much to drink, that there is no necking, that somebody plays the piano or sings during the bigger cocktail parties (thus slowing down the consumption of liquor) and that, on such occasions, the bar is shut down in ample time to speed the girls and their escorts off to an early dinner in the dining halls before the evening dance.

There is no compulsion on the part of the college that off-campus social life should be conducted under these auspices—the students apparently prefer it so. This increasing dependency on the college and its auxiliary agencies to furnish not only education but pleasure, emotional guidance, and social direction is reflected in nearly every sphere of the current Vassar life. Two hundred and sixteen Yale freshmen, for example, were imported last year by the college for a Saturday-night freshman dance—in former years the Vassar neophyte was dependent on her own initiative, the kindness of her brother or her roommate, to get herself "started." For girls from the West or from small-town high schools, this could be a source of misery, yet in my day any attempt on the part of the administration to pair us off with male wallflowers in a similar predicament was met with groans. I well remember, as a freshman member of the Vassar debate squad, being paired off with a poor freshman from Wesleyan (six and a half feet tall and chinless) when their team came to debate us on censorship and how my six roommates followed us about, laughing and drawing satirical caricatures, as we danced, ate, and walked around the campus together.

In the same way, the college's Vocational Bureau has multiplied its activities of mercy, so that the senior now who goes out into the world will be counseled, fortified, and supplied with letters of introduction by a network of Vassar alumnae. The college is a miniature welfare state. During the early thirties, a single psychiatrist, a psychologist, and a visiting consultant from Riggs Institute took care of the emotional problems of 1,250 students. Now Vassar's 1,350 girls have been endowed with a two-million-dollar grant by Paul Mellon (in memory of his wife, an alumna) for a guidance and counseling program under the direction of Dr. Carl Binger, the psychiatrist who testified in the second Alger Hiss trial.

These fresh, pink-cheeked girls in neatly turned-up blue jeans, flannel culottes, tweed jackets, well-cut shirts appear both too well adjusted and too busy to take any more guidance or counseling. The extracurricular side of Vassar life has already expanded to the point where solitude and self-questioning seem regulated out of existence. Lectures, symposia, recitals, dance programs, foreign movies compete with each other and with organized camping trips, bicycle trips, square dances, factory tours, Hall Plays, for the students' spare time. The student is always "signed up" for some activity, afternoons, evenings, weekends. There are two competing newspapers to be got out, plus the usual literary magazine, yearbook and scholarly magazine. Then there is the radio workshop, the Outing Club, the "Swupper" Club, the travel bureau. Every student is required to give four hours a week to the cooperative work program in the kitchens, dining rooms, or Message Center; slackers are put on a "blacklist" and given demerits of additional hours, which are meted out also for improper dress.

There are Student Council Meetings and Student Curriculum Committee meetings, meetings of the United World Federalists, of the Student Liberal Association, and the Students for Democratic Action. Nearly every afternoon and evening, besides the usual athletics, besides the scheduled lectures, forums, and recitals given for the college at large, there are tryouts for something or other: the Hall Play, one of the two newspapers, the literary magazine, the Flora Dora Girls, or the Gold Dusters (all Vassar music makers), the choir, the orchestra, or the Glee Club. There is scenery to be made for the Theatre (not to be confused with the Hall Plays, which are extracurricular), costumes to be sewed. There are meetings of the Thekla Club, the *Cercle Français,* the Classics Club, the Spanish Club, Philosophers' Holiday, the Psychology Club, the Russian Club, the Science Club, the German Club.

Nehru is speaking at Hyde Park; a New York doctor is discussing "Whither Medicine?" at the Dutchess County Social Planning Council; the Yale Outing Club is visiting; the Senior or Junior Prom Committee must meet; the Daisy Chain has to be chosen from the sophomore class. Founder's Day must be planned for, and the Tree Ceremonies; a note-topic is due. Jeans must be changed for dinner (only skirts are permitted in the dining room). After dinner, if no lecture or recital is impending, if there are no interviews or rehearsals, or last-minute dummying of the newspaper, if there is no reading to be done in the library, no quiz to prepare for or letters to write, there are the endless bridge and knitting in the common rooms or a hurried excursion to the Pub for beer or Cokes and conversation. And in the morning, there is the Mail Rush, the central event of the day, a jostle and scramble for love letters, letters from home, campus mail, bills, in that order of preference.

This intensification of the extracurricular life, in which every hour is planned for and assigned to some scheduled group activity, in which no one is left out or discriminated against (there are no secret societies or sororities), is the most striking feature of the current scene at Vassar. To the returning alumna whose college years were both more snobbish and sectarian, on the one hand, and more Bohemian, rebellious, and lyrical, on the other, the administrative cast, so to speak, of the present Vassar mold is both disquieting and praiseworthy. A uniform, pliant, docile undergraduate seems to be resulting from the stress on the group and the community that prevails at Vassar today. The outcast and the rebel are almost equally known. There has been a leveling-off in the Vassar geography of what was once a series of ranges, peaks, and valleys, so that Vassar, formerly known for the extremities of her climate, is now a moderate plateau. The vivid and extraordinary student, familiar to the old teachers and the alumnae, is, at least temporarily, absent from the scene.

The idea of excellence, the zest for adventure, the fastidiousness of mind and humanistic breadth of feeling that were so noticeable at Vassar during the long reign of the *emeritae* (as its retired female teachers are styled —a name that evokes a wonderful extinct species of butterfly) seem somehow to have abandoned the college, even though many of the courses that used to be given by the senior faculty have been passed on in their classic form to younger women from the graduate schools. What is missing is a certain largeness of mind, an amplitude of style, the mantle of a calling, a sense of historical dignity. I think of old Miss Haight, Elizabeth Hazelton Haight, of the Latin Department—tall, deep-voiced, Sabine, with olive skin and a mass of white hair piled high and a stately classroom delivery: her romantic attachment to Horace and Apuleius, her Augustan lecture style ("When Theseus came to Athens [pause] as it were [pause] *in medias res . . .*") and the letter she wrote the student chief justice when a group of my friends took two statues from the old Music Hall (which, together with Classics, was in the old riding academy), to celebrate with wine and garlands the opening of the new Music Building ("I regret to report the rape of Venus and Minerva from the Classics Department"). And robust, flushed, warm-hearted Anna Kitchel with her Middle-Western accent and schoolgirlish way of smoking a cigarette, which she held at a perpendicular to the orifice of her lips, puffing mightily away like a choo-choo in a child's picture book; her sympathy with George Eliot in her common-law marriage with Mr. Lewes; her sympathy with Annette, Wordsworth's abandoned light-of-love and yet her hearty relish for this un-Wordsworthian lapse ("Oh, he was a *rare bird!*"). And slight, gray-haired, pretty Helen Sandison, the Elizabethan specialist, like an Elizabethan heroine herself, with her mettlesome sharpness, her hatred of imprecision and of bowdlerization of texts. . . . At the present Vassar salary level, it is hard to attract young women fired with the ardor of teaching and capable of all the renunciations that the unmarried teacher who lives with a few books and prints in a faculty dormitory must make. For the gifted young woman today, such a life, even with summers off and sabbaticals, is not a destiny but a fate.

The problem posed by the passing of the *emeritae* is not unique, of course, to Vassar; it is felt throughout the teaching profession, wherever fine women of the old liberal school reigned—in private academies and public schools, from the big-city high school to the one-room country schoolhouse. The pioneers are gone, and who is to take their places? Other private colleges have turned to the literary avant-garde and found Abelards to substitute for the Héloïses—young male critics, philosophers, poets, novelists, short-story writers, trained, for the most part, in the New Criticism, a scholastic discipline of its own. But Vassar is committed to the *woman teacher*. That is, it considers women a discriminated-against minority in the college teaching field, and, as a woman's college, believes that it has a duty to hire women in preference to men. This principle, which worked well in the past, today creates a number of dilemmas—among them the dilemma of defining what a woman is or ought to be. Is she a childbearing animal, as some ultra-modern theorists, represented on the Vassar faculty, now contend? If so, is a spinster a woman? Is a feminist a woman? In its hiring policy, Vassar today has compromised on these questions. The faculty at present has a larger proportion of men and of married women with children than it had in former years, but now for the first time Vassar's president is a woman, and an unmarried woman, Miss Sarah Gibson Blanding, a Kentuckian, former head of the Department of Home Economics at Cornell, an economist and one-time athlete—unconventional, direct, liberal, dynamic, outspoken, hospitable. The choice of Miss Blanding a few years ago seems on the surface a victory for feminism, but at bottom it is probably a defeat. The old humanistic curriculum, which flourished under the paternal administration of President MacCracken, a Chaucerian and a classics scholar who once played Theseus in Greek for a college production of the *Hippolytus,* is slowly yielding to "education-for-living," as literature and the arts give way to the social sciences, and "pure" scholarship cedes to preparation for civic life and marriage.

Miss Blanding has gone on record as saying that college should not be "an ivory tower"; she is noted for her championship of the Negro, both in word and in deed; and Vassar, under her leadership, prides itself on its advances in social democracy. "Field work" among the people of Dutchess County is given prominence in the social sciences. The college points to the fact that, unlike most private colleges, including some progressive ones, it has no Jewish quota or geographical quota (a device for limiting, without acknowledging it, the proportion of Jewish students); it points to the three Negro girls in this year's freshman class and to the unusually high number of students recruited from public high schools, to its interdenominational church using ritual from various faiths, to its

student self-government, its fixed room rate, its cooperative work program and new cooperative dormitory, to its
interdepartmental course, *The City,* a sort of living documentary, given a few years ago under the spurring of
Helen Lockwood, the militant of sociology within the English department.

These, taken together, are indices of progress within
the field of private education, yet it must be pointed out
that the progress is relative: Vassar, after having been incorporated for more than seventy-five years, has now
achieved the degree of democracy that prevails in most
free state universities.

That maximum of social protection once afforded by
the private college to the daughters of the well-to-do is
here being withdrawn in favor of a more "open" environment that will better prepare the student for those realities of modern life that the CCNY or Hunter student faces
from birth. Meanwhile, a new questionnaire answered by
7,915 alumnae discloses that 61 per cent of those answer-
ing still favor the Republican Party and that 36 per cent
think that Vassar could have helped them "to adjust to
life" more than it did; 67 per cent, however, would choose
Vassar all over again.

The adjustment-to-life question is typical of Vassar and
perhaps, more generally, of feminine insularity and self-
centeredness—it is impossible to imagine such a question
being asked by Harvard or Chicago. But it reflects the
preoccupations of the alumnae and of certain powerful
faculty figures of the new dispensation; in particular, of
Mrs. Dorothy Lee, '27, of Anthropology, the most con-
troversial person on today's campus—dark, short-haired,
vibrant, abrupt, boyish, speaking with a slight foreign accent, photographed with her four children by the alumnae
magazine making meatballs, a cultural anthropologist of
the school that emphasizes childbearing as the crucial activity in woman's life. Careers for women in the old sense
are abhorrent to Mrs. Lee and her followers; she believes
in a faculty of homemakers, in an extension of the coop-

erative principle for training in group betterment. She detests institutional living. Her views are dynamic, integralist, and puritanical; she would sacrifice the part to the whole and believes that the one-sided person is the enemy of society. In her own way, she is a pioneer, like the spinsters who preceded her, and an iconoclast, like the suffragettes she spurns.

For the present college mood, her temper is too radical, and she is as far, perhaps, from that element in the alumnae which feels itself cheated by dishwashing and diaper-changing as from the traditionalists on the faculty who fear her influence on the students. The preparation-for-life controversy that rages in the alumnae magazine and in alumnae panel discussions reaches the undergraduate body in a somewhat muted form. The superior students do not yet demand courses in the techniques of home-making or a serious revision of the curriculum. Rather, unlike their rebellious sisters of the twenties and thirties, they look forward to "working within their community" for social betterment, while being married and having babies. As the *Vassar Alumnae Magazine* puts it, speaking of the normative Vassar woman revealed by the new questionnaire:

> She is the woman who changed the local school situation from a political machine to an educational institution. She is the woman behind the League of Women Voters, Planned Parenthood, and, yes, the 4-H Club. She won't very often be found sitting at the luncheon bridge table. She'll be found actively, thoughtfully, even serenely, playing her role as an intelligent citizen.

May, 1951

Artists in Uniform

The Colonel went out sailing,
He spoke with Turk and Jew . . .

"Pour it on, Colonel," cried the young man in the Dacron suit excitedly, making his first sortie into the club-car conversation. His face was white as Roquefort and of a glistening, cheeselike texture; he had a shock of tow-colored hair, badly cut and greasy, and a snub nose with large gray pores. Under his darting eyes were two black craters. He appeared to be under some intense nervous strain and had sat the night before in the club car drinking bourbon with beer chasers and leafing through magazines which he frowningly tossed aside, like cards into a discard heap. This morning he had come in late, with a hangdog, hangover look, and had been sitting tensely forward on a settee, smoking cigarettes and following the conversation with little twitches of the nose and quivers of the body, as a dog follows a human conversation, veering its mistrustful eyeballs from one speaker to another and raising its head eagerly at its master's voice. The colonel's voice, rich and light and plausible, had in fact abruptly risen and swollen, as he pronounced his last sentence. "I can tell you one thing," he had said harshly. "They weren't named Ryan or Murphy!"

A sort of sigh, as of consummation, ran through the club car. "Pour it on, Colonel, give it to them, Colonel, that's right, Colonel," urged the young man in a transport of admiration. The colonel fingered his collar and modest-

ly smiled. He was a thin, hawklike, black-haired handsome man with a bright blue bloodshot eye and a well-
pressed, well-tailored uniform that did not show the effects of the heat—the train, westbound for St. Louis, was
passing through Indiana, and, as usual in a heat wave, the
air-conditioning had not met the test. He wore the Air
Force insignia, and there was something in his light-boned,
spruce figure and keen, knifelike profile that suggested a
classic image of the aviator, ready to cut, piercing, into
space. In base fact, however, the colonel was in procurement, as we heard him tell the mining engineer who had
just bought him a drink. From several silken hints that
parachuted into the talk, it was patent to us that the colonel was a man who knew how to enjoy this earth and its
pleasures: he led, he gave us to think, a bachelor's life of
abstemious dissipation and well-rounded sensuality. He
had accepted the engineer's drink with a mere nod of the
glass in acknowledgment, like a genial Mars quaffing a li-
bation; there was clearly no prospect of his buying a second in return, not if the train were to travel from here
to the Mojave Desert. In the same way, an understanding
had arisen that I, the only woman in the club car, had
become the colonel's perquisite; it was taken for granted,
without an invitation's being issued, that I was to lunch
with him in St. Louis, where we each had a wait between
trains—my plans for seeing the city in a taxicab were
dished.

From the beginning, as we eyed each other over my
volume of Dickens (*"The Christmas Carol?"* suggested the
colonel, opening relations), I had guessed that the colonel
was of Irish stock, and this, I felt, gave me an advantage,
for he did not suspect the same of me; strangely so, for
I am supposed to have the map of Ireland written on my
features. In fact, he had just wagered, with a jaunty, side-
long grin at the mining engineer, that my people "came
from Boston from way back," and that I—narrowed
glance, running, like steel measuring-tape, up and down
my form—was a professional sculptress. I might have
laughed this off, as a crudely bad guess like his *Christmas*

Carol, if I had not seen the engineer nodding gravely, like an idol, and the peculiar young man bobbing his head up and down in mute applause and agreement. I was wearing a bright apple-green raw silk blouse and a dark-green rather full raw silk skirt, plus a pair of pink glass earrings; my hair was done up in a bun. It came to me, for the first time, with a sort of dawning horror, that I had begun, in the course of years, without ever guessing it, to look irrevocably Bohemian. Refracted from the three men's eyes was a strange vision of myself as an artist, through and through, stained with my occupation like the dyer's hand. All I lacked, apparently, was a pair of sandals. My sick heart sank to my Ferragamo shoes; I had always particularly preened myself on being an artist in disguise. And it was not only a question of personal vanity—it seemed to me that the writer or intellectual had a certain missionary usefulness in just such accidental gatherings as this, if he spoke not as an intellectual but as a normal member of the public. Now, thanks to the colonel, I slowly became aware that my contributions to the club-car conversation were being watched and assessed as coming from *a certain quarter.* My costume, it seemed, carefully assembled as it had been at an expensive shop, was to these observers simply a uniform that blazoned a caste and allegiance just as plainly as the colonel's khaki and eagles. *"Gardez,"* I said to myself. But, as the conversation grew tenser and I endeavored to keep cool, I began to writhe within myself, and every time I looked down, my contrasting greens seemed to be growing more and more lurid and taking on an almost menacing light, like leaves just before a storm that lift their bright undersides as the air becomes darker. We had been speaking, of course, of Russia, and I had mentioned a study that had been made at Harvard of political attitudes among Iron Curtain refugees. Suddenly, the colonel had smiled. "They're pretty Red at Harvard, I'm given to understand," he observed in a comfortable tone, while the young man twitched and quivered urgently. The eyes of all the men settled on me and waited. I flushed as I saw myself reflected. The woodland greens of my dress were turning to their complementary red, like a color-experiment in psychology or a traffic light changing. Down at the other end of the club car, a man looked up from his paper. I pulled myself together. "Set your mind at rest, Colonel," I remarked dryly. "I know Harvard very well and they're conservative to the point of dullness. The only thing crimson is the football team." This disparagement had its effect. "So . . .?" queried the colonel. "I thought there was some professor. . . ." I shook my head. "Absolutely not. There used to be a few fellow-travelers, but they're very quiet these days, when they haven't absolutely recanted. The general atmosphere is more anti-Communist than the Vatican." The colonel and the mining engineer exchanged a thoughtful stare and seemed to agree that the Delphic oracle that had just pronounced knew whereof it spoke. "Glad to hear it," said the colonel. The engineer frowned and shook his fat wattles; he was a stately, gray-haired, plump man with small hands and feet and the pampered, finical tidiness of a small-town widow. "There's so much hearsay these days," he exclaimed vexedly. "You don't know *what* to believe."

I reopened my book with an air of having closed the subject and read a paragraph three times over. I exulted to think that I had made a modest contribution to sanity in our times, and I imagined my words pyramiding like a chain letter—the colonel telling a fellow-officer on the veranda of a club in Texas, the engineer halting a works-superintendent in a Colorado mine shaft: "I met a woman on the train who claims . . . Yes, absolutely. . . ." Of course, I did not know Harvard as thoroughly as I pretended, but I forgave myself by thinking it was the convention of such club-car symposia in our positivistic country to speak from the horse's mouth.

Meanwhile, across the aisle, the engineer and the colonel continued their talk in slightly lowered voices. From time to time, the colonel's polished index-fingernail scratched his burnished black head and his knowing blue eye forayed occasionally toward me. I saw that still I was a doubtful quantity to them, a movement in the bushes, a noise, a flicker, that was figuring in their crenelated thought as "she." The subject of Reds in our colleges had not, alas, been finished; they were speaking now of another university and a woman faculty-member who had been issuing Communist statements. This story somehow, I thought angrily, had managed to appear in the newspapers without my knowledge, while these men were conversant with it; I recognized a big chink in the armor of my authority. Looking up from my book, I began to question them sharply, as though they were reporting some unheard-of natural phenomenon. "When?" I demanded. "Where did you see it? What was her name?" This request for the professor's name was a headlong attempt on my part to buttress my position, the implication being that the identities of all university professors were known to me and that if I were but given the name I could promptly clarify the matter. To admit that there was a single Communist in our academic system whose activities were hidden from me imperiled, I instinctively felt, all the small good I had done here. Moreover, in the back of my mind, I had a supreme confidence that these men were wrong: the story, I supposed, was some tattered piece of misinformation they had picked up from a gossip column. Pride, as usual, preceded my fall. To the colonel, the demand for the name was not specific but generic: what *kind* of name was the question he presumed me to be asking. "Oh," he said slowly with a luxurious yawn, "Finkelstein or Fishbein or Feinstein." He lolled back in his seat with a side glance at the engineer, who deeply nodded. There was a voluptuary pause, as the implication sank in. I bit my lip, regarding this as a mere diversionary tactic. "Please!" I said impatiently. "Can't you remember exactly?" The colonel shook his head and then his spare cheekbones suddenly reddened and he looked directly at me. "I can tell you one thing," he exclaimed irefully. "They weren't named Ryan or Murphy."

The colonel went no further; it was quite unnecessary. In an instant, the young man was at his side, yapping ex-

citedly and actually picking at the military sleeve. The
poor thing was transformed, like some creature in a fairy
tale whom a magic word releases from silence. "That's
right, Colonel," he happily repeated. "I know them. *I* was
at Harvard in the business school, studying accountancy.
I left. I couldn't take it." He threw a poisonous glance at
me, and the colonel, who had been regarding him somewhat doubtfully, now put on an alert expression and inclined an ear for his confidences. The man at the other
end of the car folded his newspaper solemnly and took a
seat by the young man's side. "They're all Reds, Colonel,"
said the young man. "They teach it in the classroom. I
came back here to Missouri. It made me sick to listen to
the stuff they handed out. If you didn't hand it back, they
flunked you. Don't let anybody tell you different." "You
are wrong," I said coldly and closed my book and rose.
The young man was still talking eagerly, and the three
men were leaning forward to catch his every gasping
word, like three astute detectives over a dying informer,
when I reached the door and cast a last look over my
shoulder at them. For an instant, the colonel's eye met
mine and I felt his scrutiny processing my green back as
I tugged open the door and met a blast of hot air, blowing my full skirt wide. Behind me, in my fancy, I saw
four sets of shrugging brows.

In my own car, I sat down, opposite two fat nuns, and
tried to assemble my thoughts. I ought to have spoken, I
felt, and yet what could I have said? It occurred to me
that the four men had perhaps not realized why I had left
the club car with such abruptness: was it possible that
they thought I was a Communist, who feared to be un-
masked? I spurned this possibility, and yet it made me
uneasy. For some reason, it troubled my *armour-propre*
to think of my anti-Communist self living on, so to speak,
green in their collective memory as a Communist or
fellow-traveler. In fact, though I did not give a fig for the
men, I hated the idea, while a few years ago I should have
counted it a great joke. This, it seemed to me, was a

measure of the change in the social climate. I had always scoffed at the notion of liberals "living in fear" of political demagoguery in America, but now I had to admit that if I was not fearful, I was at least uncomfortable in the supposition that anybody, anybody whatever, could think of me, precious me, as a Communist. A remoter possibility was, of course, that back there my departure was being ascribed to Jewishness, and this too annoyed me. I am in fact a quarter Jewish, and though I did not "hate" the idea of being taken for a Jew, I did not precisely like it, particularly under these circumstances. I wished it to be clear that I had left the club car for intellectual and principled reasons; I wanted those men to know that it was not I, but my principles, that had been offended. To let them conjecture that I had left because I was Jewish would imply that only a Jew could be affronted by an anti-Semitic outburst; a terrible idea. Aside from anything else, it voided the whole concept of transcendence, which was very close to my heart, the concept that man is more than his circumstances, more even than himself.

However you looked at the episode, I said to myself nervously, I had not acquitted myself well. I ought to have done or said something concrete and unmistakable. From this, I slid glassily to the thought that those men ought to be punished, the colonel, in particular, who occupied a responsible position. In a minute, I was framing a businesslike letter to the Chief of Staff, deploring the colonel's conduct as unbecoming to an officer and identifying him by rank and post, since unfortunately I did not know his name. Earlier in the conversation, he had passed some comments on "Harry" that bordered positively on treason, I said to myself triumphantly. A vivid image of the proceedings against him presented itself to my imagination: the long military tribunal with a row of stern soldierly faces glaring down at the colonel. I myself occupied only an inconspicuous corner of this tableau, for, to tell the truth, I did not relish the role of the witness. Perhaps it would be wiser to let the matter drop . . .? We were nearing St. Louis now; the colonel had come back into my car, and the young accountant had followed him, still talking feverishly. I pretended not to see them and turned to the two nuns, as if for sanctuary from this world and its hatred and revenges. Out of the corner of my eye, I watched the colonel, who now looked wry and restless; he shrank against the window as the young man made a place for himself amid the colonel's smart luggage and continued to express his views in a pale breathless voice. I smiled to think that the colonel was paying the piper. For the colonel, anti-Semitism was simply an aspect of urbanity, like a knowledge of hotels or women. This frantic psychopath of an accountant was serving him as a nemesis, just as the German people had been served by their psychopath, Hitler. Colonel, I adjured him, you have chosen, between him and me; measure the depth of your error and make the best of it! No intervention on my part was now necessary; justice had been meted out. Nevertheless, my heart was still throbbing violently, as if I were on the verge of some dangerous action. What was I to do, I kept asking myself, as I chatted with the nuns, if the colonel were to hold me to that lunch? And I slowly and apprehensively revolved this question, just as though it were a matter of the most serious import. It seemed to me that if I did not lunch with him—and I had no intention of doing so—I had the dreadful obligation of telling him why.

He was waiting for me as I descended the car steps. "Aren't you coming to lunch with me?" he called out and moved up to take my elbow. I began to tremble with audacity. "No," I said firmly, picking up my suitcase and draping an olive-green linen duster over my arm. "I can't lunch with you." He quirked a wiry black eyebrow. "Why not?" he said. "I understood it was all arranged." He reached for my suitcase. "No," I said, holding on to the suitcase. "I can't." I took a deep breath. "I have to tell you. I think you should be *ashamed* of yourself, Colonel, for what you said in the club car." The colonel stared: I mechanically waved for a redcap, who took my bag and coat and went off. The colonel and I stood facing each other on the emptying platform. "What do you mean?" he inquired in a low, almost clandestine tone. "Those anti-Semitic remarks," I muttered, resolutely. "You ought to be *ashamed*." The colonel gave a quick, relieved laugh. "Oh, come now," he protested. "I'm sorry," I said. "I can't have lunch with anybody who feels that way about the Jews." The colonel put down his attaché case and scratched the back of his lean neck. "Oh, come now," he repeated, with a look of amusement. "You're not Jewish, are you?" "No," I said quickly. "Well, then . . ." said the colonel, spreading his hands in a gesture of bafflement. I saw that he was truly surprised and slightly hurt by my criticism, and this made me feel wretchedly embarrassed and even apologetic, on my side, as though I had called attention to some physical defect in him, of which he himself was unconscious. "But I might have been," I stammered. "You had no way of knowing. You oughtn't to talk like that." I recognized, too late, that I was strangely reducing the whole matter to a question of etiquette: "Don't start anti-Semitic talk before making sure there are no Jews present." "Oh, hell," said the colonel, easily. "I can tell a Jew." "No, you can't," I retorted, thinking of my Jewish grandmother, for by Nazi criteria I was Jewish. "Of course I can," he insisted. "So can you." We had begun to walk down the platform side by side, disputing with a restrained passion that isolated us like a pair of lovers. All at once, the colonel halted, as though struck with a thought. "What *are* you, anyway?" he said meditatively, regarding my dark hair, green blouse, and pink earrings. Inside myself, I began to laugh. "Oh," I said gaily, playing out the trump I had been saving. "I'm Irish, like you, Colonel." "How did you know?" he said amazedly. I laughed aloud. "I can tell an Irishman," I taunted. The colonel frowned. "What's your family name?" he said brusquely. "McCarthy." He lifted an eyebrow, in defeat, and then quickly took note of my wedding ring. "That your maiden name?" I nodded. Under this peremptory questioning, I had the peculiar sensation that I get when I am lying; I began to feel that "McCarthy" was a nom de plume, a coinage of my artistic personality. But the colonel appeared to be satisfied. "Hell," he said, "come on to lunch, then. With a fine name like that, you and I should be friends." I still shook my head, though by this time we were pacing outside the station restaurant; my baggage had been checked in a locker; sweat was running down my face and I felt exhausted and hungry. I knew that I was weakening and I wanted only an excuse to yield and go inside with him. The colonel seemed to sense this. "Hell," he conceded. "You've got me wrong. I've nothing against the Jews. Back there in the club car, I was just stating a simple fact: you won't find an Irishman sounding off for the Commies. You can't deny that, can you?"

His voice rose persuasively; he took my arm. In the heat, I wilted and we went into the air-conditioned cocktail lounge. The colonel ordered two old-fashioneds. The room was dark as a cave and produced, in the midst of the hot midday, a hallucinated feeling, as though time had ceased, with the weather, and we were in eternity together. As the colonel prepared to relax, I made a tremendous effort to guide the conversation along rational, purposive lines; my only justification for being here would be to convert the colonel. "There *have* been Irishmen associated with the Communist party," I said suddenly, when the drinks came. "I can think of two." "Oh, hell," said the colonel, "every race and nation has its traitors. What I mean is, you won't find them in numbers. You've got to admit the Communists in this country are ninety per cent Jewish." "But the Jews in this country aren't ninety per cent Communist," I retorted.

As he stirred his drink, restively, I began to try to show him the reasons why the Communist movement in America had attracted such a large number, relatively, of Jews: how the Communists had been anti-Nazi when nobody else seemed to care what happened to the Jews in Germany; how the Communists still capitalized on a Jewish fear of fascism; how many Jews had become, after Buchenwald, traumatized by this fear. . . .

But the colonel was scarcely listening. An impatient frown rested on his jaunty features. "I don't get it," he said slowly. "Why should you be for them, with a name like yours?" "I'm *not* for the Communists," I cried. "I'm just trying to explain to you—" "For the Jews," the colonel interrupted, irritable now himself. "I've heard of such people but I never met one before." "I'm not 'for' them," I protested. "You don't understand. I'm not for *any* race or nation. I'm against those who are against them." This word, *them,* with a sort of slurring circle drawn round it, was beginning to sound ugly to me. Automatically, in arguing with him, I seemed to have slipped into the colonel's style of thought. It occurred to me that defense of the Jews could be a subtle and safe form of anti-Semitism, an exercise of patronage: as a rational Gentile, one could feel superior both to the Jews and the anti-Semites. There could be no doubt that the Jewish question evoked a curious stealthy lust or concupiscence. I could feel it now vibrating between us over the dark table. If I had been a good person, I should unquestionably have got up and left.

"I don't get it," repeated the colonel. "How were you brought up? Were your people this way too?" It was manifest that an odd reversal had taken place; each of us regarded the other as "abnormal" and was attempting to understand the etiology of a disease. "Many of my people think just as you do," I said, smiling coldly. "It seems to be a sickness to which the Irish are prone. Perhaps it's due to the potato diet," I said sweetly, having divined that the colonel came from a social stratum somewhat lower than my own.

But the colonel's hide was tough. "You've got me wrong," he reiterated, with an almost plaintive laugh. "I don't dislike the Jews. I've got a lot of Jewish friends. Among themselves, they think just as I do, mark my words. I tell you what it is," he added ruminatively, with a thoughtful prod of his muddler, "I draw a distinction between a kike and a Jew." I groaned. "Colonel, I've never heard an anti-Semite who didn't draw that distinction. You know what Otto Kahn said? 'A kike is a Jewish gentleman who has just left the room.' " The colonel did not laugh. "I don't hold it against some of them," he persisted, in a tone of pensive justice. "It's not their fault if they were born that way. That's what I tell them, and they respect me for my honesty. I've had a lot of discussions; in procurement, you have to do business with them, and the Jews are the first to admit that you'll find more chiselers among their race than among the rest of mankind." "It's not a race," I interjected wearily, but the colonel pressed on. "If I deal with a Jewish manufacturer, I can't bank on his word. I've seen it again and again, every damned time. When I deal with a Gentile, I can trust him to make delivery as promised. That's the difference between the two races. They're just a different breed. They don't have standards of honesty, even among each other." I sighed, feeling unequal to arguing the colonel's personal experience.

"Look," I said, "you may be dealing with an industry where the Jewish manufacturers are the most recent comers and feel they have to cut corners to compete with the established firms. I've heard that said about Jewish cattle-dealers, who are supposed to be extra sharp. But what I think, really, is that you notice it when a Jewish firm fails to meet an agreement and don't notice it when it's a Yankee." "Hah," said the colonel. "They'll tell you what I'm telling you themselves, if you get to know them and go into their homes. You won't believe it, but some of my best friends are Jews," he said, simply and thoughtfully, with an air of originality. "They may be *your* best friends, Colonel," I retorted, "but you are not theirs. I defy you to tell me that you talk to them as you're talking now." "Sure," said the colonel, easily. "More or less." "They must be very queer Jews you know," I observed tartly, and I began to wonder whether there indeed existed a peculiar class of Jews whose function in life was to be "friends" with such people as the colonel. It was difficult to think that all the anti-Semites

who made the colonel's assertion were the victims of a
cruel self-deception.

A dispirited silence followed. I was not one of those
liberals who believed that the Jews, alone among peoples,
possessed no characteristics whatever of a distinguishing
nature—this would mean they had no history and no culture, a charge which should be leveled against them only
by an anti-Semite. Certainly, types of Jews could be noted
and patterns of Jewish thought and feeling: Jewish humor,
Jewish rationality, and so on, not that every Jew reflected
every attribute of Jewish life or history. But somehow,
with the colonel, I dared not concede that there was such
a thing as a Jew: I saw the sad meaning of the assertion
that a Jew was a person whom other people thought was
Jewish.

Hopeless, however, to convey this to the colonel. The
desolate truth was that the colonel was extremely stupid,
and it came to me, as we sat there, glumly ordering lunch,
that for extremely stupid people anti-Semitism was a
form of intellectuality, the sole form of intellectuality of
which they were capable. It represented, in a rudimentary
way, the ability to make categories, to generalize. Hence
a thing I had noted before but never understood: the
fact that anti-Semitic statements were generally delivered
in an atmosphere of profundity. Furrowed brows attended
these speculative distinctions between a kike and a Jew,
these little empirical laws that you can't know one without knowing them all. To arrive, indeed, at the idea of a
Jew was, for these grouping minds, an exercise in Platonic
thought, a discovery of essence, and to be able to add
the great corollary, "Some of my best friends are Jews,"
was to find the philosopher's cleft between essence and
existence. From this, it would seem, followed the querulous
obstinacy with which the anti-Semite clung to his concept;
to be deprived of this intellectual tool by missionaries of
tolerance would be, for persons like the colonel, the
equivalent of Western man's losing the syllogism: a lapse
into animal darkness. In the club car, we had just witnessed an example: the colonel with his anti-Semitic ob-

servation had come to the mute young man like the paraclete, bearing the gift of tongues.

Here in the bar, it grew plainer and plainer that the colonel did not regard himself as an anti-Semite but merely as a heavy thinker. The idea that I considered him anti-Semitic sincerely outraged his feelings. "Prejudice" was the last trait he could have imputed to himself. He looked on me, almost respectfully, as a "Jew-lover," a kind of being he had heard of but never actually encountered, like a centaur or a Siamese twin, and the interest of relating this prodigy to the natural state of mankind overrode any personal distaste. There I sat, the exception which was "proving" or testing the rule, and he kept pressing me for details of my history that might explain my deviation in terms of the norm. On my side, of course, I had become fiercely resolved that he would learn nothing from me that would make it possible for him to dismiss my anti-anti-Semitism as the product of special circumstances: I was stubbornly sitting on the fact of my Jewish grandmother like a hen on a golden egg. I was bent on making *him* see himself as a monster, a deviation, a heretic from Church and State. Unfortunately, the colonel, owing perhaps to his military training, had not the glimmering of an idea of what democracy meant; to him, it was simply a slogan that was sometimes useful in war. The notion of an ordained inequality was to him "scientific."

"Honestly," he was saying in lowered tones, as our drinks were taken away and the waitress set down my sandwich and his corned-beef hash, "don't you, brought up the way you were, feel about them the way I do? Just between ourselves, isn't there a sort of inborn feeling of horror that the very word, Jew, suggests?" I shook my head, roundly. The idea of an *innate* anti-Semitism was in keeping with the rest of the colonel's thought, yet it shocked me more than anything he had yet said. "No," I sharply replied. "It doesn't evoke any feeling one way or the other." "Honest Injun?" said the colonel. "Think back; when you were a kid, didn't the word, Jew, make you feel sick?" There was a dreadful sincerity about this that made me answer in an almost kindly tone. "No, truthfully, I assure you. When we were children, we learned to call the old-clothes man a sheeny, but that was just a dirty word to us, like 'Hun' that we used to call after workmen we thought were Germans."

"I don't get it," pondered the colonel, eating a pickle. "There must be something wrong with you. Everybody is born with that feeling. It's natural; it's part of nature." "On the contrary," I said. "It's something very unnatural that you must have been taught as a child." "It's not something you're *taught*," he protested. "You must have been," I said. "You simply don't remember it. In any case, you're a man now; you must rid yourself of that feeling. It's psychopathic, like that horrible young man on the train." "You thought he was crazy?" mused the colonel, in an idle, dreamy tone. I shrugged my shoulders. "Of course. Think of his color. He was probably just out of a mental institution. People don't get that tattletale gray except in prison or mental hospitals." The colonel suddenly grinned. "You might be right," he said. "He was quite a case." He chuckled.

I leaned forward. "You know, Colonel," I said quickly, "anti-Semitism is contrary to the Church's teaching. God will make you do penance for hating the Jews. Ask your priest; he'll tell you I'm right. You'll have a long spell in Purgatory, if you don't rid yourself of this sin. It's a deliberate violation of Christ's commandment, 'Love thy neighbor.' The Church holds that the Jews have a sacred place in God's design. Mary was a Jew and Christ was a Jew. The Jews are under God's special protection. The Church teaches that the millennium can't come until the conversion of the Jews; therefore, the Jews must be preserved that the Divine Will may be accomplished. Woe to them that harm them, for they controvert God's Will!" In the course of speaking, I had swept myself away with the solemnity of the doctrine. The Great Reconciliation between God and His chosen people, as envisioned by the Evangelist, had for me at that moment a piercing, majestic beauty, like some awesome Tintoretto. I saw a noble spectacle of blue sky, thronged with gray clouds, and a vast white desert, across which God and Israel advanced to meet each other, while below in hell the demons of disunion shrieked and gnashed their teeth.

"Hell," said the colonel, jovially, "I don't believe in all that. I lost my faith when I was a kid. I saw that all this God stuff was a lot of bushwa." I gazed at him in stupefaction. His confidence had completely returned. The blue eyes glittered debonairly, the eagles glittered; the narrow polished head cocked and listened to itself like a trilling bird. I was up against an airman with a bird's-eye view, a man who believed in nothing but the law of kind: the epitome of godless materialism. "You still don't hold with that bunk?" the colonel inquired in an undertone, with an expression of stealthy curiosity. "No," I confessed, sad to admit to a meeting of minds. "You know what got me?" exclaimed the colonel. "That birth-control stuff. Didn't it kill you?" I made a neutral sound. "I was beginning to play around," said the colonel, with a significant beam of the eye, "and I just couldn't take that guff. When I saw through the birth-control talk, I saw through the whole thing. They claimed it was against nature, but I claim, if that's so, an operation's against nature. I told my old man that when he was having his kidney stones out. You ought to have heard him yell!" A rich, reminiscent satisfaction dwelt in the colonel's face.

This period of his life, in which he had thrown off the claims of the spiritual and adopted a practical approach, was evidently one of those "turning points" to which a man looks back with pride. He lingered over the story of his break with church and parents with a curious sort of heat, as though the flames of old sexual conquests stirred within his body at the memory of those old quarrels. The looks he rested on me, as a sharer of that experience, grew more and more lickerish and assaying. "What got *you* down?" he finally inquired, settling

back in his chair and pushing his coffee cup aside. "Oh,"
I said wearily, "it's a long story. You can read it when
it's published." "You're an author?" cried the colonel, who
was really very slow-witted. I nodded, and the colonel
regarded me afresh. "What do you write? Love stories?"
He gave a half-wink. "No," I said. "Various things. Articles. Books. Highbrowish stories." A suspicion darkened
in the colonel's sharp face. "That McCarthy," he said. "Is
that your pen name?" "Yes," I said, "but it's my real
name too. It's the name I write under *and* my maiden
name." The colonel digested this thought. "Oh," he con-
cluded.

A new idea seemed to visit him. Quite cruelly, I
watched it take possession. He was thinking of the power
of the press and the indiscretions of other military figures,
who had been rewarded with demotion. The consciousness of the uniform he wore appeared to seep uneasily
into his body. He straightened his shoulders and called
thoughtfully for the check. We paid in silence, the colonel
making no effort to forestall my dive into my pocket-
book. I should not have let him pay in any case, but it
startled me that he did not try to do so, if only for
reasons of vanity. The whole business of paying, apparently, was painful to him; I watched his facial muscles contract as he pocketed the change and slipped two dimes
for the waitress onto the table, not daring quite to hide
them under the coffee cup—he had short-changed me on
the bill and the tip, and we both knew it. We walked
out into the steaming station and I took my baggage out
of the checking locker. The colonel carried my suitcase
and we strolled along without speaking. Again, I felt horribly embarrassed for him. He was meditative, and I supposed that he too was mortified by his meanness about
the tip.

"Don't get me wrong," he said suddenly, setting the
suitcase down and turning squarely to face me, as
though he had taken a big decision. "I may have said a
few things back there about the Jews getting what they
deserved in Germany." I looked at him in surprise; ac-

tually, he had not said that to me. Perhaps he had let it drop in the club car after I had left. "But that doesn't mean I approve of Hitler." "I should hope not," I said. "What I mean is," said the colonel, "that they probably gave the Germans a lot of provocation, but that doesn't excuse what Hitler did." "No," I said, somewhat ironically, but the colonel was unaware of anything satiric in the air. His face was grave and determined; he was sorting out his philosophy for the record. "I mean, I don't approve of his methods," he finally stated. "No," I agreed. "You mean, you don't approve of the gas chamber." The colonel shook his head very severely. "Absolutely not! That was terrible." He shuddered and drew out a handkerchief and slowly wiped his brow. "For God's sake," he said, "don't get me wrong. I think they're human beings." "Yes," I assented, and we walked along to my track. The colonel's spirits lifted, as though, having stated his credo, he had both got himself in line with public policy and achieved an autonomous thought. "I mean," he resumed, "you may not care for them, but that's not the same as killing them, in cold blood, like that." "No, Colonel," I said.

He swung my bag onto the car's platform and I climbed up behind it. He stood below, smiling, with upturned face. "I'll look for your article," he cried, as the train whistle blew. I nodded, and the colonel waved, and I could not stop myself from waving back at him and even giving him the corner of a smile. After all, I said to myself, looking down at him, the colonel was "a human being." There followed one of those inane intervals in which one prays for the train to leave. We both glanced at our watches. "See you some time," he called. "What's your married name?" "Broadwater," I called back. The whistle blew again. "Brodwater?" shouted the colonel, with a dazed look of unbelief and growing enlightenment; he was not the first person to hear it as a Jewish name, on the model of Goldwater. "B-r-o-a-d," I began, automatically, but then I stopped. I disdained to spell it out for him; the victory was his. "One of the chosen, eh?" his brief grimace seemed to commiserate. For the last time, and in the final fullness of understanding, the hawk eye patrolled the green dress, the duster, and the earrings; the narrow flue of his nostril contracted as he curtly turned away. The train commenced to move.

March, 1953

Settling the Colonel's Hash

Seven years ago, when I taught in a progressive college, I had a pretty girl student in one of my classes who wanted to be a short-story writer. She was not studying writing with me, but she knew that I sometimes wrote short stories, and one day, breathless and glowing, she came up to me in the hall, to tell me that she had just written a story that her writing teacher, a Mr. Converse, was terribly excited about. "He thinks it's wonderful," she said, "and he's going to help me fix it up for publication."

I asked what the story was about; the girl was a rather simple being who loved clothes and dates. Her answer had a deprecating tone. It was just about a girl (herself) and some sailors she had met on the train. But then her face, which had looked perturbed for a moment, gladdened.

"Mr. Converse is going over it with me and we're going to put in the symbols."

Another girl in the same college, when asked by us in her sophomore orals why she read novels (one of the pseudo-profound questions that ought never to be put) answered in a defensive flurry: "Well, *of course* I don't read them to find out what happens to the hero."

At the time, I thought these notions were peculiar to

This was given first as a talk at the Breadloaf School of English, in Middlebury, Vermont. Cf. "Artists in Uniform," page 68.

progressive education: it was old-fashioned or regressive
to read a novel to find out what happens to the hero or
to have a mere experience empty of symbolic pointers.
But I now discover that this attitude is quite general,
and that readers and students all over the country are in
a state of apprehension, lest they read a book or story
literally and miss the presence of a symbol. And like
everything in America, this search for meanings has become a socially competitive enterprise; the best reader is
the one who detects the most symbols in a given stretch
of prose. And the benighted reader who fails to find any
symbols humbly assents when they are pointed out to
him; he accepts his mortification.

I had no idea how far this process had gone until last
spring, when I began to get responses to a story I had
published in *Harper's*. I say "story" because that was
what it was called by *Harper's*. I myself would not know
quite what to call it; it was a piece of reporting or a
fragment of autobiography—an account of my meeting
with an anti-Semitic army colonel. It began in the club
car of a train going to St. Louis; I was wearing an apple-
green shirtwaist and a dark-green skirt and pink earrings;
we got into an argument about the Jews. The colonel
was a rather dapper, flashy kind of Irish-American with
a worldly blue eye; he took me, he said, for a sculptress,
which made me feel, to my horror, that I looked Bohemian and therefore rather suspect. He was full of the
usual profound clichés that anti-Semites air, like original
epigrams, about the Jews: that he could tell a Jew, that
they were different from other people, that you couldn't
trust them in business, that some of his best friends were
Jews, that he distinguished between a Jew and a kike,
and finally that, of course, he didn't agree with Hitler:
Hitler went too far; the Jews were human beings.

All the time we talked, and I defended the Jews, he was
trying to get my angle, as he called it; he thought it was
abnormal for anybody who wasn't Jewish not to feel as he
did. As a matter of fact, I have a Jewish grandmother,
but I decided to keep this news to myself: I did not want

the colonel to think that I had any interested reason for speaking on behalf of the Jews, that is, that I was prejudiced. In the end, though, I got my comeuppance. Just as we were parting, the colonel asked me my married name, which is Broadwater, and the whole mystery was cleared up for him, instantly; he supposed I was married to a Jew and that the name was spelled B-r-o-d-w-a-t-e-r. I did not try to enlighten him; I let him think what he wanted; in a certain sense, he was right; he had unearthed my Jewish grandmother or her equivalent. There were a few details that I must mention to make the next part clear: in my car, there were two nuns, whom I talked to as a distraction from the colonel and the moral problems he raised. He and I finally had lunch together in the St. Louis railroad station, where we continued the discussion. It was a very hot day. I had a sandwich; he had roast-beef hash. We both had an old-fashioned.

The whole point of this "story" was that it really happened; it is written in the first person; I speak of myself in my own name, McCarthy; at the end, I mention my husband's name, Broadwater. When I was thinking about writing the story, I decided not to treat it fictionally; the chief interest, I felt, lay in the fact that it happened, in real life, last summer, to the writer herself, who was a good deal at fault in the incident. I wanted to embarrass myself and, if possible, the reader too.

Yet, strangely enough, many of my readers preferred to think of this account as fiction. I still meet people who ask me, confidentially, "That story of yours about the colonel—was it really true?" It seemed to them perfectly natural that I would write a fabrication, in which I figured under my own name, and sign it, though in my eyes this would be like perjuring yourself in court or forging checks. Shortly after the "story" was published, I got a kindly letter from a man in Mexico, in which he criticized the menu from an artistic point of view: he thought salads would be better for hot weather and it would be more in character for the narrator-heroine to have a martini. I did not answer the letter, though I was moved to, because I had the sense that he would not understand the distinction between what *ought* to have happened and what *did* happen.

Then in April I got another letter, from an English teacher in a small college in the Middle West, that reduced me to despair. I am going to cite it at length.

"My students in freshman English chose to analyze your story, 'Artists in Uniform,' from the March issue of *Harper's*. For a week I heard oral discussions on it and then the students wrote critical analyses. In so far as it is possible, I stayed out of their discussions, encouraging them to read the story closely with your intentions as a guide to their understanding. Although some of them insisted that the story has no other level than the realistic one, most of them decided it has symbolic overtones.

"The question is: how closely do you want the symbols labeled? They wrestled with the nuns, the author's two shades of green with pink accents, with the 'materialistic godlessness' of the colonel. . . . A surprising number wanted exact symbols; for example, they searched for the significance of the colonel's eating hash and the author eating a sandwich. . . . From my standpoint, the story was an entirely satisfactory springboard for understanding the various shades of prejudice, for seeing how much of the artist goes into his painting. If it is any satisfaction to you, our campus was alive with discussions about 'Artists in Uniform.' We liked the story and we thought it amazing that an author could succeed in making readers dislike the author—for a purpose, of course!"

I probably should have answered this letter, but I did not. The gulf seemed to me too wide. I could not applaud the backward students who insisted that the story has no other level than the realistic one without giving offense to their teacher, who was evidently a well-meaning person. But I shall try now to address a reply, not to this teacher and her unfortunate class, but to a whole school

of misunderstanding. There were no symbols in this story;
there was no deeper level. The nuns were in the story
because they were on the train; the contrasting greens
were the dress I happened to be wearing; the colonel had
hash because he had hash; materialistic godlessness meant
just what it means when a priest thunders it from the
pulpit—the phrase, for the first time, had meaning for
me as I watched and listened to the colonel.

But to clarify the misunderstanding, one must go a
little further and try to see what a literary symbol is.
Now in one sense, the colonel's hash and my sandwich
can be regarded as symbols; that is, they typify the colonel's food tastes and mine. (The man in Mexico had
different food tastes which he wished to interpose into our
reality.) The hash and the sandwich might even be said
to show something very obvious about our characters
and bringing-up, or about our sexes; I was a woman, he
was a man. And though on another day I might have
ordered hash myself, that day I did not, because the
colonel and I, in our disagreement, were polarizing each
other.

The hash and the sandwich, then, could be regarded as
symbols of our disagreement, almost conscious symbols.
And underneath our discussion of the Jews, there was a
thin sexual current running, as there always is in such
random encounters or pickups (for they have a strong
suggestion of the illicit). The fact that I ordered something
conventionally feminine and he ordered something conventionally masculine represented, no doubt, our awareness of a sexual possibility; even though I was not attracted to the colonel, nor he to me, the circumstances of
our meeting made us define ourselves as a woman and a
man.

The sandwich and the hash were our provisional, *ad
hoc* symbols of ourselves. But in this sense all human
actions are symbolic because they represent the person
who does them. If the colonel had ordered a fruit salad
with whipped cream, this too would have represented

him in some way; given his other traits, it would have pointed to a complexity in his character that the hash did not suggest.

In the same way, the contrasting greens of my dress were a symbol of my taste in clothes and hence representative of me—all too representative, I suddenly saw, in the club car, when I got an "artistic" image of myself flashed back at me from the men's eyes. I had no wish to stylize myself as an artist, that is, to parade about as a symbol of flamboyant unconventionality, but apparently I had done so unwittingly when I picked those colors off a rack, under the impression that they suited me or "expressed my personality" as salesladies say.

My dress, then, was a symbol of the perplexity I found myself in with the colonel; I did not want to be categorized as a member of a peculiar minority—an artist or a Jew; but brute fate and the colonel kept resolutely cramming me into both those uncomfortable pigeonholes. I wished to be regarded as ordinary or rather as universal, to be anybody and therefore everybody (that is, in one sense, I wanted to be on the colonel's side, majestically above minorities); but every time the colonel looked at my dress and me in it with my pink earrings I shrank to minority status, and felt the dress in the heat shriveling me, like the shirt of Nessus, the centaur, that consumed Hercules.

But this is not what the students meant when they wanted the symbols "labeled." They were searching for a more recondite significance than that afforded by the trite symbolism of ordinary life, in which a dress is a social badge. They supposed that I was engaging in literary or artificial symbolism, which would lead the reader out of the confines of reality into the vast fairy tale of myth, in which the color green would have an emblematic meaning (or did the two greens signify for them what the teacher calls "shades" of prejudice), and the colonel's hash, I imagine, would be some sort of Eucharistic mincemeat.

Apparently, the presence of the nuns assured them

there were overtones of theology; it did not occur to
them (a) that the nuns were there because pairs of nuns
are a standardized feature of summer Pullman travel, like
crying babies, and perspiring businessmen in the club car,
and (b) that if I thought the nuns worth mentioning, it
was also because of something very simple and directly
relevant: the nuns and the colonel and I all had something in common—we had all at one time been Catholics
—and I was seeking common ground with the colonel,
from which to turn and attack his position.

In any account of reality, even a televised one, which
comes closest to being a literal transcript or replay,
some details are left out as irrelevant (though nothing is
really irrelevant). The details that are not eliminated
have to stand as symbols of the whole, like steno-
graphic signs, and of course there is an art of selection,
even in a newspaper account: the writer, if he has any
ability, is looking for the revealing detail that will sum up
the picture for the reader in a flash of recognition.

But the art of abridgment and condensation, which is
familiar to anybody who tries to relate an anecdote, or
give a direction—the art of natural symbolism, which is
at the basis of speech and all representation—has at
bottom a centripetal intention. It hovers over an object,
and event, or series of events and tries to declare what
it is. Analogy (that is, comparison to other objects) is
inevitably one of its methods. "The weather was soupy,"
i.e., like soup. "He wedged his way in," i.e., he had to
enter, thin edge first, as a wedge enters, and so on. All
this is obvious. But these metaphorical aids to communication are a far cry from literary symbolism, as taught in
the schools and practiced by certain fashionable writers.
Literary symbolism is centrifugal and flees from the object, the event, into the incorporeal distance, where con-
cepts are taken for substance and floating ideas and
archetypes assume a hieratic authority.

In this dream-forest, symbols become arbitrary; all
counters are interchangeable; anything can stand for

anything else. The colonel's hash can be a Eucharist or a cannibal feast or the banquet of Atreus, or all three, so long as the actual dish set before the actual man is disparaged. What is depressing about this insistent symbolization is the fact that while it claims to lead to the infinite, it quickly reaches very finite limits—there are only so many myths on record, and once you have got through Bulfinch, the Scandinavian, and the Indian, there is not much left. And if all stories reduce themselves to myth and symbol, qualitative differences vanish, and there is only a single, monotonous story.

American fiction of the symbolist school demonstrates this mournful truth, without precisely intending to. A few years ago, when the mode was at its height, chic novels and stories fell into three classes: those which had a Greek myth for their framework, which the reader was supposed to detect, like finding the faces in the clouds in old newspaper puzzle contests; those which had symbolic modern figures, dwarfs, hermaphrodites, and cripples, illustrating maiming and loneliness; and those which contained symbolic animals, cougars, wild cats, and monkeys. One young novelist, a product of the Princeton school of symbolism, had all three elements going at once, like the ringmaster of a three-ring circus, with the freaks, the animals, and the statues.

The quest for symbolic referents had as its object, of course, the deepening of the writer's subject and the reader's awareness. But the result was paradoxical. At the very moment when American writing was penetrated by the symbolic urge, it ceased to be able to create symbols of its own. Babbitt, I suppose, was the last important symbol to be created by an American writer; he gave his name to a type that henceforth would be recognizable to everybody. He passed into the language. The same thing could be said, perhaps, though to a lesser degree, of Caldwell's Tobacco Road, Eliot's Prufrock, and possibly of Faulkner's Snopeses. The discovery of new symbols is not the only function of a writer, but the writer who cares about this must be fascinated by reality itself, as a butterfly collector is fascinated by the glimpse of a new specimen. Such a specimen was Mme. Bovary or M. Homais or M. de Charlus or Jupien; these specimens were precious to their discoverers, not because they repeated an age-old pattern but because their markings were new. Once the specimen has been described, the public instantly spots other examples of the kind, and the world seems suddenly full of Babbitts and Charlus, where none had been noted before.

A different matter was Joyce's Mr. Bloom. Mr. Bloom can be called a symbol of eternal recurrence—the wandering Jew, Ulysses the voyager—but he is a symbol thickly incarnate, fleshed out in a Dublin advertising canvasser. He is not *like* Ulysses or vaguely suggestive of Ulysses; he is Ulysses, circa 1905. Joyce evidently believed in a cyclical theory of history, in which everything repeated itself; he also subscribed in youth to the doctrine that declares that the Host, a piece of bread, is also God's body and blood. How it can be both things at the same time, transubstantially, is a mystery, and Mr. Bloom is just such a mystery: Ulysses in the visible appearance of a Dublin advertising canvasser.

Mr. Bloom is not a symbol of Ulysses, but Ulysses-Bloom together, one and indivisible, symbolize or rather demonstrate eternal recurrence. I hope I make myself clear. The point is transubstantiation: Bloom and Ulysses are transfused into each other and neither reality is diminished. Both realities are locked together, like the protons and neutrons of an atom. *Finnegans Wake* is a still more ambitious attempt to create a fusion, this time a myriad fusion, and to exemplify the mystery of how a thing can be itself and at the same time be something else. The world is many and it is also one.

But the clarity and tension of Joyce's thought brought him closer in a way to the strictness of allegory than to the diffuse practices of latter-day symbolists. In Joyce, the equivalences and analogies are very sharp and distinct, as in a pun, and the real world is almost querulously audible, like the voices of the washerwomen on the Liffey

that come into Earwicker's dream. But this is not true of
Joyce's imitators or of the imitators of his imitators, for
whom reality is only a shadowy pretext for the introduction of a whole *corps de ballet* of dancing symbols in
mythic draperies and animal skins.

Let me make a distinction. There are some great writers, like Joyce or Melville, who have consciously introduced symbolic elements into their work; and there are
great writers who have written fables or allegories. In
both cases, the writer makes it quite clear to the reader
how he is to be read; only an idiot would take *Pilgrim's
Progress* for a realistic story, and even a young boy,
reading *Moby Dick,* realizes that there is something more
than whale-fishing here, though he may not be able to
name what it is. But the great body of fiction contains
only what I have called natural symbolism, in which
selected events represent or typify a problem, a kind of
society or psychology, a philosophical theory, in the same
way that they do in real life. What happens to the hero
becomes of the highest importance. This symbolism needs
no abstruse interpretation, and abstruse interpretation
will only lead the reader away from the reality that the
writer is trying to press on his attention.

I shall give an example or two of what I mean by
natural symbolism and I shall begin with a rather florid
one: Henry James' *The Golden Bowl.* This is the story of
a rich American girl who collects European objects. One
of these objects is a husband, Prince Amerigo, who
proves to be unfaithful. Early in the story, there is a visit
to an antique shop in which the Prince picks out a gold
bowl for his fiancée and finds, to his annoyance, that
it is cracked. It is not hard to see that the cracked bowl
is a symbol, both of the Prince himself, who is a valuable
antique but a little flawed, morally, and also of the marriage, which represents an act of acquisition or purchase
on the part of the heroine and her father. If the reader
should fail to notice the analogy, James calls his attention
to it in the title.

I myself would not regard this symbol as necessary to

this particular history; it seems to me, rather, an ornament of the kind that was fashionable in the architecture
and interior decoration of the period, like stylized sheaves
of corn or palms on the façade of a house. Nevertheless, it is handsome and has an obvious appropriateness
to the theme. It introduces the reader into the Gilded
Age attitudes of the novel. I think there is also a scriptural
echo in the title that conveys the idea of punishment. But
having seen and felt the weight of meaning that James
put into this symbol, one must not be tempted to press
further and look at the bowl as a female sex symbol, a
chalice, a Holy Grail, and so on; a book is not a pious
excuse for reciting a litany of associations.

My second example is from Tolstoy's *Anna Karenina*.
Toward the beginning of the novel, Anna meets the
man who will be her lover, Vronsky, on the Moscow-St.
Petersburg express; as they meet, there has been an accident; a workman has been killed by the train. This is
the beginning of Anna's doom, which is completed when
she throws herself under a train and is killed; and the
last we see of Vronsky is in a train, with a toothache; he
is off to the wars. The train is necessary to the plot of
the novel, and I believe it is also symbolic, both of the
iron forces of material progress that Tolstoy hated so
and that played a part in Anna's moral destruction, and
also of those iron laws of necessity and consequence
that govern human action when it remains on the sensual
level.

One can read the whole novel, however, without being
conscious that the train is a symbol; we do not have to
"interpret" to feel the import of doom and loneliness in
the train's whistle—the same import we ourselves can
feel when we hear a train whistle blow in the country,
even today. Tolstoy was a deeper artist than James, and
we cannot be sure that the train was a conscious device
with him. The appropriateness to Anna's history may
have been only a *felt* appropriateness; everything in Tolstoy has such a supreme naturalness that one shrinks

from attributing contrivance to him, as if it were a sort of fraud. Yet he worked very hard on his novels—I forget how many times Countess Tolstoy copied out *War and Peace* by hand.

The impression one gets from his diaries is that he wrote by ear; he speaks repeatedly, even as an old man, of having to start a story over again because he has the wrong tone, and I suspect that he did not think of the train as a symbol but that it sounded "right" to him, because it was, in that day, an almost fearsome emblem of ruthless and impersonal force, not only to a writer of genius but to the poorest peasant in the fields. And in Tolstoy's case I think it would be impossible, even for the most fanciful critic, to extricate the train from the novel and try to make it say something that the novel itself does not say directly. Every detail in Tolstoy has an almost cruel and viselike meaningfulness and truth to itself that make it tautological to talk of symbolism; he was a moralist and to him the tiniest action, even the curiosities of physical appearance, Vronsky's bald spot, the small white hands of Prince Andrei, told a moral tale.

It is now considered very old-fashioned and tasteless to speak of an author's "philosophy of life" as something that can be harvested from his work. Actually, most of the great authors did have a "philosophy of life" which they were eager to communicate to the public; this was one of their motives for writing. And to disentangle a moral philosophy from a work that evidently contains one is far less damaging to the author's purpose and the integrity of his art than to violate his imagery by symbol-hunting, as though reading a novel were a sort of paper-chase.

The images of a novel or a story belong, as it were, to a family, very closely knit and inseparable from each other; the parent "idea" of a story or a novel generates events and images all bearing a strong family resemblance. And to understand a story or a novel, you must look for the parent "idea," which is usually in plain view, if you read quite carefully and literally what the author says.

I will go back, for a moment, to my own story, to show how this can be done. Clearly, it is about the Jewish question, for that is what the people are talking about. It also seems to be about artists, since the title is "Artists in Uniform." Then there must be some relation between artists and Jews. What is it? They are both minorities that other people claim to be able to recognize by their appearance. But artists and Jews do not care for this categorization; they want to be universal, that is, like everybody else. They do not want to wear their destiny as a badge, as the soldier wears his uniform. But this aim is really hopeless, for life has formed them as Jews or artists, in a way that immediately betrays them to the majority they are trying to melt into. In my conversation with the colonel, I was endeavoring to play a double game. I was trying to force him into a minority by treating anti-Semitism as an aberration, which, in fact, I believe it is. On his side, the colonel resisted this attempt and tried to show that anti-Semitism was normal, and he was normal, while I was the queer one. He declined to be categorized as anti-Semite; he regarded himself as an independent thinker, who by a happy chance thought the same as everybody else.

I imagined I had a card up my sleeve; I had guessed that the colonel was Irish (i.e., that he belonged to a minority) and presumed that he was a Catholic. I did not see how he could possibly guess that I, with my Irish name and Irish appearance, had a Jewish grandmother in the background. Therefore when I found I had not convinced him by reasoning, I played my last card; I told him that the Church, his Church, forbade anti-Semitism. I went even further; I implied that God forbade it, though I had no right to do this, since I did not believe in God, but was only using Him as a whip to crack over the colonel, to make him feel humble and inferior, a raw Irish Catholic lad under discipline. But the colonel, it turned out, did not believe in God, either, and I lost. And since, in a sense, I had been cheating all along in this game we were playing, I had to concede the colonel a sort of moral victory in the end; I let him think that my husband was Jewish and that that "explained" everything satisfactorily.

Now there are a number of morals or meanings in this little tale, starting with the simple one: don't talk to strangers on a train. The chief moral or meaning (what I learned, in other words, from this experience) was this: you cannot be a universal unless you accept the fact that you are a singular, that is, a Jew or an artist or what-have-you. What the colonel and I were discussing, and at the same time illustrating and enacting, was the definition of a human being. I was trying to be something better than a human being; I was trying to be the voice of pure reason; and pride went before a fall. The colonel, without trying, was being something worse than a human being, and somehow we found ourselves on the same plane—facing each other, like mutually repellent twins. Or, put in another way: it is dangerous to be drawn into discussions of the Jews with anti-Semites: you delude yourself that you are spreading light, but you are really sinking into muck; if you endeavor to be dispassionate, you are really claiming for yourself a privileged position, a little mountain top, from which you look down, impartially, on both the Jews and the colonel.

Anti-Semitism is a horrible disease from which nobody is immune, and it has a kind of evil fascination that makes an enlightened person draw near the source of infection, supposedly in a scientific spirit, but really to sniff the vapors and dally with the possibility. The enlightened person who lunches with the colonel in order, as she tells herself, to improve him, is cheating herself, having her cake and eating it. This attempted cheat, on my part, was related to the question of the artist and the green dress; I wanted to be an artist but not to pay the price of looking like one, just as I was willing to have Jewish blood but not willing to show it, where it would cost me something— the loss of superiority in an argument.

These meanings are all there, quite patent, to anyone who consents to look *into* the story. They were *in* the experience itself, waiting to be found and considered. I did not perceive them all at the time the experience was happening; otherwise, it would not have taken place, in all probability—I should have given the colonel a wide berth. But when I went back over the experience, in order to write it, I came upon these meanings, protruding at me, as it were, from the details of the occasion. I put in the green dress and my mortification over it because they were part of the truth, just as it had occurred, but I did not see how they were related to the general question of anti-Semitism and my grandmother until they *showed* me their relation in the course of writing.

Every short story, at least for me, is a little act of discovery. A cluster of details presents itself to my scrutiny, like a mystery that I will understand in the course of writing or sometimes not fully until afterward, when, if I have been honest and listened to these details carefully, I will find that they are connected and that there is a coherent pattern. This pattern is *in* experience itself; you do not impose it from the outside and if you try to, you will find that the story is taking the wrong tack, dribbling away from you into artificiality or inconsequence. A story that you do not learn something from while you are writing it, that does not illuminate something for you, is dead, finished before you started it. The "idea" of a story is implicit in it, on the one hand; on the other hand, it is always ahead of the writer, like a form dimly discerned in the distance; he is working *toward* the "idea."

It can sometimes happen that you begin a story thinking that you know the "idea" of it and find, when you are finished, that you have said something quite different and utterly unexpected to you. Most writers have been haunted all their lives by the "idea" of a story or a novel that they think they want to write and see very clearly: Tolstoy always wanted to write a novel about the Decembrists and instead, almost against his will, wrote *War and Peace;* Henry James thought he wanted to write a novel about Napoleon. Probably these ideas for novels were too set in their creators' minds to inspire creative discovery.

In any work that is truly creative, I believe, the writer cannot be omniscient in advance about the effects that he proposes to produce. The suspense in a novel is not only in the reader, but in the novelist himself, who is intensely curious too about what will happen to the hero. Jane Austen may know in a general way that Emma will marry Mr. Knightley in the end (the reader knows this too, as a matter of fact); the suspense for the author lies in the how, in the twists and turns of circumstance, waiting but as yet unknown, that will bring the consummation about. Hence, I would say to the student of writing that outlines, patterns, arrangements of symbols may have a certain usefulness at the outset for some kinds of minds, but in the end they will have to be scrapped. If the story does not contradict the outline, overrun the pattern, break the symbols, like an insurrection against authority, it is surely a stillbirth. The natural symbolism of reality has more messages to communicate than the dry Morse code of the disengaged mind.

The tree of life, said Hegel, is greener than the tree of thought; I have quoted this before but I cannot forbear from citing it again in this context. This is not an incitement to mindlessness or an endorsement of realism in the short story (there are several kinds of reality, including interior reality); it means only that the writer must be, first of all, a listener and observer, who can pay attention to reality, like an obedient pupil, and who is willing, always, to be surprised by the messages reality is sending through to him. And if he gets the messages correctly he will not have to go back and put in the symbols; he will find that the symbols are there, staring at him significantly from the commonplace.

February, 1954

A New Word

1956—1958: LONDON

At first glance, the main actors in *Look Back in Anger* appear to be three newspapers and an ironing-board. When the curtain goes up, on a cheap one-room flat, the audience sees a pair of Sunday papers, a cloud of pipe-smoke, and some men's feet and legs protruding; more papers are scattered on the floor, and, off to one side, a woman is silently ironing a shirt. "Why do I do this every Sunday?" exclaims Jimmy Porter, throwing his paper down. "Even the book reviews seem to be the same as last week's. Different books—same reviews." At the rise of the third-act curtain, months later, the two male figures are still enveloped in the Sunday papers, while a woman is silently ironing a shirt. Same scene—different girl. Nothing really changes; nothing can change. That is the horror of Sunday. Jimmy's wife, Alison, a colonel's daughter, has finally left him, but her girl-friend, Helena, has stepped into her shoes. Jimmy, a working-class intellectual, still has a hostage from the ruling class doing the washing and the cooking, and his friend, Cliff, an uneducated Welsh boy, who boards with them, is still looking on. There has been a swap of upper-class women, like the swap of posh newspapers: you put down *The Observer* and pick up *The Sunday Times*—same contents, different make-up. A blonde is replaced by a brunette, and there is a different set of make-up on the dressing-table. The two "class" newspapers, one Liberal, one Tory, are interchangeable, and the mass newspaper, *The News of the World,* is a weekly Psychopathia Sexualis. Other fixtures in the cast of characters are some church bells outside, the unseen landlady downstairs, and a storage-tank in the middle of the flat that represents Jimmy Porter's mother-in-law—in the third act, the new girl at the ironing-board, a homemaker, has put a slip-cover on "Mummy," which does not alter the fact that Mummy is still present, built in to the apartment, as she is built in to English life.

The stagnant boredom of Sundays in a provincial town, with the pubs closed and nothing to do but read the papers, is a travesty of the day of rest—the day which officially belongs to the private person, who is here seen as half an inert object and half a restless phantom staring through the bars of his prison. Nobody can deny that this feeling of being pent-up is characteristic of Sunday, perhaps for the majority of people in Anglo-Saxon countries. Jimmy Porter is still young enough to feel that something *ought* to happen, something a little different, to break the monotony. He believes that Sunday has a duty to be interesting. John Osborne's critics, on the contrary, believe that Jimmy has a duty not to be bored or at least not to show it, not to keep talking about it. As Helena, who marches into the play waving the standard of criticism, tells her friend Alison, Jimmy will have to learn to behave like everybody else.

"Why can't you be like other people?" This extreme demand, which always rises to the surface in quarrels between married couples, leaps from behind the footlights to confront Jimmy Porter; the play alerts a kind of intimate antagonism in its audiences, as though audience and hero were a wedded pair, headed straight for the divorce court, recriminations, lawyers, ugly charges. Criticism has picked the play to pieces, as though it were a trumped-up story; imagined discrepancies or improbabilities are pounced on ("The play is not true to life; people do their ironing on Mondays," or "They would have finished reading the papers by four o'clock in the after-

noon"). One critic, writing in *The New Republic,* thinks
he knows why Jimmy Porter can't be like other people:
homosexual tendencies. Nor would Jimmy Porter, if he
could reply, change a single feature of his conduct to
avoid the drawing of this inference. The play almost asks
to be misunderstood, like an infuriated, wounded person;
out of bravado, it coldly refuses to justify itself.

Jimmy Porter's boredom is a badge of freedom, and he
will not be passive about it; for him, boredom is a positive
activity, a proclamation. To be actively, angrily, militantly
bored is one of the few forms of protest open to him that
do not compromise his independence and honesty. At the
same time it is one of the few forms of recreation he can
afford; his boredom becomes an instrument on which he
plays variations, as he does on his trumpet in the next
room. But other people suffer, it is said. He ought not to
make other people suffer because *he* is unhappy and out
of sorts. No doubt, but this is unfortunately the way unhappy people are; they are driven to distribute the suffering.

For Jimmy Porter, moreover, there is a principle involved. He is determined to stay alive, which means that
he must struggle against the soporific substitutes for real
life that make up the Sunday program: the steady soft
thud of the iron and the regular rustle of newsprint. His
friend, Cliff, keeps telling him to shut up; his badgered
wife, Alison, only wants peace, a little peace, but that is
what Jimmy, or a part of Jimmy, his needling, cruel voice,
has decided that she shall not have. He is fighting to keep
her awake, to keep himself and his friend awake, as
though all three were in the grip of a deathly coma or
narcosis that had been spread over all of England by the
gases emanating from the press, the clergy, the political
parties, the B.B.C. Jimmy Porter's gibes are a therapeutic
method designed to keep a few people alive, whether they
like it or not, and patterned on the violent procedures
used with patients who have taken an overdose of drugs
and whose muttered plea, like Alison's, is always to be
left alone.

This, at any rate, is what Jimmy thinks he is doing. His voice is a calculated irritant that prevents the other characters from lapsing into torpor. For his own part, he is tired of listening to himself and would be glad to tune in on another station, where something was really happening, where there was a little enthusiasm; he would like, some time, just once, to hear "a warm, thrilling voice cry out Hallelujah!" Instead, there is only the deadly static provided by the Sunday weeklies, the Bishop of Bromley blessing the hydrogen bomb, and the church bells ringing outside. He thinks he would like to listen to a concert of Vaughan Williams's music, but the ironing interferes with the reception, and he irritably shuts the radio off.

"Interference" is what Jimmy detests, whether it comes from the iron, his mother-in-law, his wife's girl-friend, or the church bells. He is morbidly suspicious in any case and morbidly sensitive to "foreign" noises. At the same time, he is unnerved by silence. The only sound he really trusts is the sound of his own voice, which he keeps turned on mechanically, almost absently, as other people keep a phonograph going. This voice is very droll and funny, which is how it placates censure; it is "as good as a show." But the other characters sometimes plead with Jimmy to be quiet; they cannot "hear themselves think" or read the papers in peace or go on with the ironing because of that voice. And if it stops talking, it moves into the next room and starts blowing on a trumpet. It never runs down and when it seems to flag for a moment, it is only to gather fresh energy, like a phonograph that pauses to let the record turn over. Jimmy demands an undivided attention, even when he is absent, and he is quick to know when no one is listening. "I'm sorry; I wasn't listening properly," says Alison at the beginning of the play. "You bet you weren't listening," he retorts. "Old Porter talks and everyone turns over and goes to sleep. And Mrs. Porter gets 'em going with the first yawn."

Behind all this is more than egotism or a childish insistence on being the center of the stage. Jimmy Porter is a completely isolated person whose profoundest, quickest,

most natural instinct is mistrust. This is the automatic,
animal wariness of a creature that feels itself surrounded.
Solidarity, a working-class virtue, is for him the only virtue that is real; he exacts complete allegiance and fealty
from anyone who enters his life. His women appear, so to
speak, wearing his colors; both girls, while they *are* his,
are seen wearing one of his old shirts over their regular
clothes. When Alison is found in a slip, dressing to go
out, in the second act, this is proof that she is about to
revert, away from him, back to her own kind. Jimmy
would make his women into men if he could, *not* because
he is a covert homosexual, but because, if they were men,
he could trust them. Women do not have that natural
quality of solidarity that exists between men, and they
have always been suspected by men for precisely this reason; women live in the artificial realm of the social and
are adepts at transferring allegiances ("making new
friends") and at all the arts of deception and camouflage
of which the dressing-table, stage left, is the visible sign.
Alison lets Jimmy down at the crucial moment of the play
—a thing he finds unthinkable, as does Alison's father,
Colonel Redfern. This is followed, appropriately, by another betrayal: Alison's girl-friend, Helena, seizes Jimmy
for herself.

The story of *Look Back in Anger* has, from this point
of view, a great deal in common with *Hamlet*. Cliff, the
working-class Welsh boy, is Jimmy Porter's Horatio, who
sticks to him without understanding all the fine points of
Jimmy's philosophy; and the scenes Jimmy makes with
Alison have the same candid brutality that Hamlet showed
to Ophelia. In both cases, the frenzied mockery springs
from an expectation of betrayal. Ophelia is felt to be the
ally of the corrupt Court with the murderer-king at its
head, of her dull brother, Laertes, and her father, that
ass Polonius. In *Look Back in Anger,* brother Nigel is
Laertes and Alison's mother is cast in the role of Polonius, lurking behind the arras. The fact that Alison is se-
cretly exchanging letters with her means that she is in
communication with the enemy, like that other docile

daughter, Ophelia. Women cannot be trusted because they do not understand that such an act is treachery; they do it "in all innocence." Apart from anything else, they do not take in the meaning of a declaration of war.

Both Hamlet and Jimmy Porter have declared war on a rotten society; both have been unfitted by a higher education from accepting their normal place in the world. They think too much and criticize too freely. Jimmy, like Hamlet, might have become a species of courtier or social sycophant; that is, he might have "got ahead." Critics complain that he ought to have found a job at a provincial university, instead of torturing himself and his nice wife by running a sweet stall. Hamlet, too, might have settled down to a soft berth in the Court of Denmark, married Ophelia, and waited for the succession. Hamlet's tirades and asides are plainly calculated to disturb and annoy the Court. He too cannot stop talking and, like Jimmy Porter, who practises vaudeville routines, he turns to the players for relief from the "real" world of craft, cunning, and stupidity. Both heroes are naturally histrionic, and in both cases the estrangement, marked by histrionics, is close at moments to insanity. Both have no fixed purpose beyond that of awakening the people around them from their trance of acceptance and obliging them to be conscious of the horror and baseness of the world. Both (though this is clearer in Hamlet's case) suffer from a horrible self-doubt that alternates with wild flashes of conviction, and neither wholly wills the events he himself is causing. Yet neither wants to repent whatever it is that is driving him to destroy everything in sight, and both repel pity. "He wouldn't *let* me pity him," said a young woman, sadly, coming out of *Look Back in Anger*. That is just the concession the play refuses to make; if the audience pitied Jimmy Porter, this would be interference.

The Entertainer is a softer play than *Look Back in Anger*. The enemy here is identified with the "men of Suez" and the right wing generally; this, being a political grievance, is easier for the audience to sympathize with. To be angry about politics is conventional. The Suez crisis is somewhat arbitrarily linked with a family of music-hall performers whose contact with the invasion is so remote, theatrically, that the fact that they have a son "out there," fighting, is only mentioned, like an afterthought, at the end of the third scene. On the surface, this play has far more plot than *Look Back in Anger:* Archie Rice, a down-and-out music-hall comedian, is pursued by bankruptcy and the figure of the Income Tax man; he wants to leave his old, sodden, moronic wife and marry a young girl; his daughter goes to the Trafalgar Square protest meeting against Suez and breaks her engagement; his father dies; his other son and probably his wife are going off to Canada to join some relations, while he is slated for jail. Yet much of this plot is clumsily messengered in, by telegrams, newspaper stories, straight narration, so that it seems a kind of dubious hearsay—the daughter's engagement to someone called "Graham"; the young girl they say Archie wants to marry; even the two deaths. The relations in Canada come to life, if life it can be called in the letter that is read from them describing their TV set and their new Chevrolet Bel-Air. This is enough to tell Archie that he would rather go to jail, and it is enough for the audience to get the picture in a flash. But, with this exception, nothing that occurs on the periphery carries much conviction; the center is Archie Rice, lit by a spot, standing before a curtain gamely doing his act, while beyond him, in the wings, there is only an empty blackness, a void of shadows. Somewhere in that void there is the Man with the Hook—death and taxes.

Jimmy Porter is "as good as a show," and Archie, with his tipped hat and bow tie and gloves and cane and blackened eyebrows, is the grisly show itself. He is the eternal performer who enters before the variety queens and who has to hold the audience or else be jerked off the stage. His function is to keep the show going, no matter what— if a fire breaks out or the bombs start falling or somebody dies. Like Jimmy, Archie cannot stop talking; this is his professional misfortune—the commitment he has made to the management. Silence, for this old pro, is the ultimate

terror; he listens intently, head cocked, for the laugh or
the patter of applause rising from the darkness of the pit,
to assure him that he is still there, in the spotlight, in
short that he still exists. If his own voice falters, if he
dries up, he is done for; the orchestra will strike up to
cover the silence, and the hook will come out to claim
him. All the clichés of the stage, of the old trouper who
"never missed a performance," take on in this play a
quality of sheer horror.

The actor and the soldier have the same mythology;
timing, co-ordination, a cool nerve, resourcefulness, are
essential to the discipline. A vaudevillian like Archie Rice
looks on the stage as a fort he is holding, until relief in
the form of the next turn will appear. Before a performance every actor experiences a slight case of battle-nerves,
and actors, like soldiers, are superstitious. In *The Entertainer* this equation between the actor and the soldier is
instinctively caught and exploited for an effect of tragic
pathos. The link with Suez seems strained in terms of
stage-plotting, while the characters are merely talking and
drinking gin, like other people. But when Archie, in costume, is revealed with a tall nude behind him, like a recruiting poster, who wears the helmet of Britannia and
holds a bulldog and a trident, the grotesque relation becomes real. His fading personal fortunes are eerily identified with the fading of the Empire. His personal hollowness echoes the present hollowness of the Empire idea,
and the proposed retreat to Canada signifies the shift of
power. The old growling bulldog England is represented
by Archie's father, an old trouper and veteran who went
through the Dardanelles without a scratch and who re-
enlists, as it were, when summoned by Archie to save the
family's collective life; he dies at his post, performing, and
his coffin is draped in the Union Jack. The old man's
sacrifice, to save a "no-good, washed-up, tatty show," is a
useless expenditure. The silence that Archie fears closes
in at the end; it is the death of old England. The actor is
finished, and it is the audience's turn to "have a go."

"Don't clap too hard, we're all in a very old building"—

this grim antique vaudeville wheeze which is part of Archie's stock of gags evokes another play, written at another crisis of the declining Empire, during the First World War: Shaw's *Heartbreak House*. Shaw's draughty old country house, England, which is run by a mad, drunken sea-captain, has gone down still another step with John Osborne, and become a draughty old vaudeville house at a run-down coastal resort, with an alcoholic comedian introducing a girl-show. Shaw was a man of sixty when he wrote *Heartbreak House*, and Osborne was twenty-eight, last year, when *The Entertainer* was first produced. Both men had received a bitter education in the school of poverty that made the protected assumptions of well-to-do people appear to them as a kind of ludicrous insanity. Shaw's father was a drunkard; Osborne's mother was a barmaid. Shaw got his training for the stage as a speaker at street-corners and socialist meetings; Osborne got his as an actor, often unemployed. Bravado, impatience of cant, and a gift of gab are the product of these experiences. Shaw, to the day of his death, was obsessed with waking people up, rubbing their noses in the raw facts of life, of which they seemed so incredibly ignorant; Osborne is the same, though somewhat more savage, having come from lower down in the social scale. Shaw was, of course, an inveterate entertainer; that was his calamity, like Archie Rice's. And, like Jimmy Porter, he could never give his public a rest, leave them in peace to read the paper; he was always "at" them, telling them their faults, just as he did with his friends. The audience, toward the end, got a little tired of him, and he, no doubt, got a little tired of himself, coming on to do his turn, in his grizzled stage eyebrows and beard. More and more, as he grew older, he had the feeling that he was talking sense and no one was listening.

Throughout both John Osborne's plays there is a longing for a message, a "new word"—for purification, simplification. Personally, like Shaw, he is a vegetarian and does not drink alcohol. Shaw thought he had a message, if he could only get people to hear it. Osborne is in a more radical fix. Shaw could not sell him simplified spelling or an easy way to socialism. There is no new word, and, if there were, nobody would listen. One of Archie Rice's sons is a conscientious objector, but he has no hope of converting anyone and does not try; being a c.o. is his way of being an odd-ball, in a family of odd-balls, and he accepts it for that, as one accepts one's face. Archie Rice's daughter has been giving art lessons to a gang of tough kids in a London Youth Club; she does not expect any good to come of it. Yet she has been moved by the Trafalgar Square meeting to the point where she feels that something *might* happen, something in fact *must* happen, some change or redemption. Hence she comes home and starts trying to redeem Archie. But Archie is way ahead of her—a nice man, friendly, but far beyond recall, off in lunar space, where no new word could reach him. The transparent gauzes and dissolving walls of the stage set explain what has happened to the home the girl has come back to and which she takes for solid. It is a transparent deception; you can see straight through it, out into the blackness. This ectoplasm of a home is inhabited by monologists; nobody listens, as the girl and the old man protest; everyone tells the same story, airs the same objections, like a collection of tired phonographs. The voices are slurred and they forget what they started to say; there was a point to be made, long ago, but it has been forgotten.

Archie, the head of this dissolving household, has been dead a long time and floated off into filmy unreal distances, beyond the pull of gravity, with the spotlight still playing on him, picking him out, like some powerful telescope. Nothing can happen to Archie any more because he is a spook, dead, as he says, behind the eyes. Archie is in eternity, steadily doing his routine, grinding out his grinning patter, like the salt mill that fell into the sea ("You wouldn't think I was sexy to look at me, would you? No, honestly, would you, lady?"). He has heard something once (the "warm, thrilling voice"), an old Negress singing, but he was half-stewed at the time, so that his account of the message is garbled. Now he half-listens to his daughter, politely, warily, trying to get her point of view, that is, to fix the remote point in space where this new sound is coming from. Archie is not always certain when he is onstage and when he is at home; it is all a cover-up anyway. He may be dead, but he is not taken in. The last story he tells, in his final stage appearance, is a story about a little man who finds himself in eternity, in paradise, and when a saint on the welcoming committee asks him what he thinks of it, he looks around the upper regions and answers with a four-letter word. After a moment's consternation, the saint throws his arms around the little man and kisses him. He has been waiting to hear that word ever since he came there —that is, for all eternity.

What is that word, exactly? And what has John Osborne got against Heaven? The answer is very simple. The word is hell (h-e-l-l), and that is what John Osborne has to say about this other-Eden, demi-paradise, the Welfare State, where, as Archie observes ironically, "nobody wants, and nobody goes without, all are provided for." The anger of John Osborne, which has angered so many people, is total and uncompromising; these two plays are nothing more or less than lively descriptions of hell. Those who want to be told what is biting the playwright have only to look around them, at the general fatuity and emptiness which is so much taken for granted that it appears as normal and almost no one hopes or wishes for anything better. A good deal has been made of the fact that Osborne, in an essay published in a volume called *Declaration*, attacked the Queen and the Tories; but the Queen, as admirers of royalty are fond of pointing out, is only a symbol anyway, a symbol of the universal cover-up in which the Tories co-operate, but not the Tories alone. Osborne is no Labour-Party canvasser, offering false teeth and nationalized steel to the masses; the changes which might be effected, under present conditions, by a return of Labour to power would be minute, and Osborne knows this. To have Labour in power would make a tiny difference, a break in the monotony; a *little* reality might filter in. Osborne is a socialist who prefers working-class people to people who have never seen a flat with an outside toilet for the same reason that Shaw did: because, on the whole, they are more real; because, like Candida's father and Eliza Doolittle's father, they are shameless and unregenerate observers of what goes on around them. Sixty or seventy years ago, when Shaw began writing, such a preference appeared less shocking and mystifying than it does today, which itself is a proof that it was time someone spoke out again, plainly, and let the sound of a human voice, now evidently so unfamiliar, rattle the old building.

Odd Man In

A TOUCH OF THE POET. EUGENE O'NEILL.
HELEN HAYES THEATER.
EPITAPH FOR GEORGE DILLON. JOHN OSBORNE
AND ANTHONY CREIGHTON.
JOHN GOLDEN THEATER.
DEATHWATCH. JEAN GENÊT. THEATER EAST.

A drunkard, an unemployed actor, and a petty criminal are the non-heroes of these new plays, all written by men of real talent in a mode of defiant honesty that has come to be their professional signature. Each deals with a *mauvais sujet* who is also a painful subject, and each is tense with a lyrical rhetoric of confession and self-exposure that at times amounts to hysteria, embarrassing to the audience, which, not being trained as a priestly confessor, regards the stage revelations as an attack. More and more today, the theater at its most serious is becoming an arena of combat with the audience; arena theater or theater-in-the-round is not just a presentational gimmick but a style of writing that involves the spectator as an unwilling accessory and that works just as well when the proscenium arch is kept.

The non-hero as a disturbing central figure had already been discovered by Chekhov, in the early play, *Ivanov,* now running at the Renata Theatre. Nothing Chekhov did later is as radical as this study. Uncle Vanya is ineffectual and the novelist Trigorin is a middling sensual man, but their non-heroic qualities are seen in a softened and palliated light: "Well, it's only human nature," a neighbor might philosophize of their conduct. This is not true of Ivanov, a very strange man, sallow, nervous, good-looking, sensitive, fond of reading, without evident vices, who is

ruining his property and the lives and characters of everyone around him by an inner demoralization. He is married to a tubercular Jewess, whom he once loved and
who is now just such a febrile, melancholy invalid as a
provincial doctor, like Chekhov, might see regularly on his
rounds. Ivanov's family doctor has told him, repeatedly,
that his course of conduct is literally killing his wife:
the inability to settle down to anything, to stay home for
a single evening or put any kind of order into his affairs.
Ivanov feels compunction without being able to change.
You would think, comments the spectator, that he could
be nice to her for a few hours at least, under the circumstances. But no, he cannot. It is off to the town in a
buggy—to a vulgar provincial salon that bores him. And
yet he is not a villain—only not a hero; Chekhov, a realist,
takes pains to show that it would require actual heroism
for this restless person to spend a few hours with his
ailing wife. Invalids are trying to be with. But just this
allowance that Chekhov, as an experienced doctor, makes
for Ivanov renders the character highly disturbing to the
audience. Is he excusable or isn't he? Or, as the audience
keeps arguing during the intermission, is he supposed to
be "sympathetic"?

The audience, furthermore, could be reconciled to
Ivanov if it were assured that he was the victim of a
complex or a typical product of a social environment and
hence "determined," an effect of a known cause. But no
explanation is forthcoming; it really is not clear why this
man is falling to pieces. All that is plain is that Ivanov
cannot control his actions, that his actions are indeed
the reverse of what he would will them to be. His behavior is a doom or tic to which he is subject without
being altered in his inner nature. A liberal of emanci-
pated views, he commits the unforgivable sin, at a climactic point of the plot, of taunting his sick wife with
being Jewish; this sin, just because it is unforgivable, has
been waiting for him all along, as though it were endowed
with consciousness and had only to bide its time for him
to commit it—at the most unforgivable moment. "Why

did you have to say that *then*?" the audience, appalled, wants to shriek at him. "You know the poor woman is dying." But the truth is that the cry "Jewess!" had to leap out of him at the very instant when he would least consent to utter it, when, in other words, it could not be taken back. And having gone this far, Ivanov goes still further in shamelessness; he lets her know what the doctor had been keeping from her, the facts of her condition.

After such knowledge, what forgiveness? Ivanov has done the unpardonable and yet he is not even a villain. This position is the very essence of the non-heroic. It is not the immortal gods that have been offended but Ivanov's conception of himself as an educated, civilized gentleman who would not do precisely what he has just done. This sensitive conception feels pain, and in that very idea there is naturally something ludicrous. "Forgive me, Nora; that was unpardonable," says Major Con Melody in *A Touch of the Poet,* apologizing to his wife for an ugly statement that "slipped out." Almost immediately, he does it again. "Deeply moved," he kisses her and then suddenly pushes her away. "For God's sake, why don't you wash your hair? It turns my stomach with its stink of onions and stew." And once more: "Forgive me, Nora." This is Jimmy Porter, all over, in *Look Back in Anger:* "Darling, I'm sorry. . . . I'm sorry. . . . I mean it." Such jerky, inconsonant behavior, like the twitching of a nerve, is found in all the non-heroes of the modern stage, in James Tyrone of *Long Day's Journey into Night,* Jimmy, Archie Rice of *The Entertainer,* Lefranc, the petty thief of *Deathwatch,* as well as Ivanov, George Dillon, and Con Melody. They carry the unpardonable to its furthest limits, and yet in themselves they do not appear to be sufficient cause for what they do, even though, in fact, they may be directly responsible for the death or destruction of another person: Ivanov for the death of his wife, James Tyrone for the drug-addiction of *his* wife and the near-death of his son, Jimmy for the death of Alison's unborn child, Archie for the death of his father, Lefranc for the murder of Maurice, a harmless seventeen-year-old punk. Their actions do not make them great, even in a criminal sense, because their actions are somehow inexpressive of who they are, and many of these non-heroes require a forgiving woman who claims to "understand."

Of the three new plays, Jean Genêt's *Deathwatch* is the coldest examination of the non-hero, because the scene is laid, not in conventional society where "forgiveness" and "understanding" are readily accorded and have to be (otherwise, there would be no getting on), but in a prison cell, where an inflexible code prevails. The criminal code is one of strict rank: a killer rates highest and a pickpocket or housebreaker is lowest on the scale. Multiple crimes of immense daring (e.g., sensational daylight holdups) may be matched against the beauty of a single exquisite killing; and other factors, such as the amount of newspaper publicity, the length and breadth of the manhunt, and the demeanor of the accused when captured, are taken into consideration. These standards, at which the audience laughs, are taken very seriously by the prisoners and the guards, who are concerned with definitions of greatness: which is greater, the Negro called Snowball (never seen onstage), whose crimes include the holdup of a gold train, or Green Eyes, who has killed a little girl? In reality, the atmosphere of Genêt's prison is remarkably like that of a big-city American high school, with its football and basketball heroes, secret societies, crushes, jealousies, favoritism, and interracial tension. "Snowball is exotic," boasts Lefranc at the beginning, excited because the big Negro has smiled at him in the corridor that morning. Nevertheless, those who laugh at all this are probably being philistines, from Genêt's point of view: they are people who laugh at a poem. "Snowball is black, but he dazzles," says Lefranc, and Green Eyes shines in the cell like a steady burning jewel, quickening in Lefranc, a small-time thief and liar, an impulse to rob him of his glory, that is, to become his equal by committing a murder of his own. He strangles Maurice, Green Eyes's lover, the third occupant of the cell. But he is not "big" enough for his action, which remains a mere inert byproduct of his petty will and thieving ambition. "What am I going to do? Green Eyes, help me," he cries out, and Green Eyes replies, "*I* help you? You disgust me. To rub out a boy who hadn't done a thing. For nothing. For glory. . . . You disgust me." Green Eyes, a natural being, had not wanted his own unnatural crime; it had chosen him, singled him out as he walked down the street with a sprig of lilac in his teeth. God or the devil had presented him with his "glory," a dubious gift, that had caused him much suffering to accept. In the words of society, he has paid for his crime. Lefranc's misunderstanding of all this is what keeps him from belonging, from being accepted in the prison, even by the guards. "You are right. I am really alone," says Lefranc as the curtain falls.

Lefranc, though not an artist in crime, is an artist in words; he has been writing Green Eyes's letters to his wife. "I am the post office," he says at one point, recalling Joyce's Shem the Postman. The word-artist is the permanent outsider; even the humblest criminals, like Maurice, will not accept him as one of them. For John Osborne in *Epitaph for George Dillon*, it is the shabby smallness of George Dillon that marks him straight off for an artist. You would know he was some sort of actor or writer (actually, he is both) because of his long rather greasy hair, with the forelock hanging down, hungry, ferret face, sleepy gait, selfishness, and mooching habits; added to this, he is a vegetarian, speaks in an educated voice, and tells lies. No ordinary person could be as awful as George, and he is half-persuaded of this himself. The very word, *actor*, which is what he is, strikes him as derisory and shameful. Toward ordinary people, among whom he is thrown by necessity, his attitude is one of mingled contempt and stark wonder. A brisk, sentimental, lower-middle-class woman, Mrs. Elliot, has brought him home from the office to live with her family because she "believes" in him and his future; to George, her belief is at once grotesque and wonderful. She identifies him, quite

illusorily, with her son, who was killed in the war and
whose room George moves into as a non-paying boarder.
"You stupid-looking bastard," exclaims George violently,
as soon as he is left alone with the cherished son's photo.

The saddest part about George—the source of confu-
sion—is that he is not altogether a faker. The play he
has been writing improbably gets produced, after it has
been edited to suit the popular taste. He becomes, in
the end, a success, which was what he and Mrs. Elliot
wanted for him, but being a "success" is the ultimate
absurd ignominy. "Turned out to be Bernard Shaw, after
all, eh?" says Mrs. Elliot's husband, Percy, contemplat-
ing the box office returns; George, in short, has compelled
the admiration of "a small, mean little man" by the vulgarity of making good. He has moved, like a clown, from
the cliché of failure to the platitude of success, and indeed he is trapped in clichés and platitudes, detected by
his ear but beyond the power of his will to escape from,
like the hideous furniture—the cocktail cabinet, the "contemporary" chair, the telly, and the painting of ducks in
flight ("those blasted birds")—of the Elliot home. George
had "hoped, thought he was that mysterious, ridiculous
being called an artist"; instead, he finds himself written
into a script of his own creation, which has him having
to marry the younger Elliot daughter, whom, incredibly, he
has got in the family way. "Incredibly," "improbably"—
that is the way things happen to George; either he is
real to himself and outside events are therefore incredible
because they seem to have no connection with him, or
vice versa: the events are real and he, amidst them, is
the improbability.

It cannot be a coincidence that all three of the current non-heroes are fish out of water—educated men
confined with illiterates or the nearest thing to it—and
that all three, as if to emphasize their false position, are
liars. To the Elliot family (Percy Elliot excepted), George
is always a gentleman, that is, a superior order of person
entitled to superior consideration. This is only another
way of saying that George, to them, is an artist; seen from

below, the two appear to be the same thing. In the prison world of *Deathwatch,* such illusions do not exist, and Lefranc's superior education makes him, if anything, suspicious to his cellmates. But in *A Touch of the Poet,* as the title indicates, you again find an artist-gentleman profiting with a bad conscience from the respect of the uncultured. Major Cornelius Melody, late of the Duke of Wellington's service in the Peninsular War, now a derelict tavernkeeper in New England, is worshipped and coddled as an aristocrat by his low-born, rheumatic drudge of a wife, who wears herself out in the inn so that he can keep a thoroughbred mare in the barn, spout passages of Lord Byron, and once a year put on his fine red uniform to celebrate at a drunken dinner the anniversary of the Battle of Talavera. He and George are really museum-pieces kept in the house by the lower orders and tenderly brushed and polished; this is vividly symbolized by O'Neill in the red uniform of the British Army officer that is brought down from the trunk ceremonially every July 27 for the ruined Irish major to posture inside of. But like so many home-preserved museum-pieces, the major is of doubtful authenticity. He is not an aristocrat but the son of a new-rich peasant; his army career was genuine, like the bit of anguished truth in George, but, by the time the play opens, Con Melody is nothing but a seamy drunkard living off the sweaty labor of others, whom he despises for their smell. The major's excuse is that, again like George, he has a finer consciousness—a touch of the poet. Moreover, the protective museum-atmosphere that surrounds him is a prison, allowing him no freedom to be what he actually is; it is his wife and daughter who press him to go upstairs and put on his uniform. The major and George are half-unwilling actors performing at the request of the pit. Their lies and semi-truths are bolstered by other lies—the shock-absorbent cushions of the unlettered. "It was the liquor talking," says Nora, explaining Con away, even though everyone else in his establishment knows that Con means what he says but did not mean to say it . . . exactly.

The notion of a gentleman, above all of a poet-gentleman, cuts two ways. If it implies ready, soothing forgiveness on the part of the lower orders, it also implies that there are certain things a gentleman cannot do and be forgiven—at any rate by himself. Education and sensitivity are supposed, by those who have them, to constitute some sort of guarantee or safeguard; that, in fact, they do not is the terrible and banal discovery of the non-hero. He cannot, as they say, live with himself afterwards. The shock of hearing himself transgress the limits of what he feels to be civilized conduct is almost too much for Ivanov: he cannot be the person he thought he was. This is what happens to Green Eyes, 22 years old, handsome, and analphabetic, when the lurid crime he commits fastens itself on him like another, strange identity with which he must become reconciled before he can become a god, one of "les grands, les durs." But for the educated semi-gentleman, no other identity, including that of a god, is socially possible. "Live with himself *socially*" is what is meant. Neither Ivanov nor George Dillon nor Con Melody can tolerate his own shameless company.

What recourse is left to them? Ivanov, who is about to be married to a young girl, shoots himself instead. The title of the Osborne play, *Epitaph for George Dillon*, suggests that Mr. Osborne has finally got rid of Dillon, a bad lot. In the last act of the O'Neill play, a shot is heard, and the audience, together with Con's wife and daughter, assumes that he has killed himself. No such luck for him; he has only shot his beautiful mare, the sign of his lying pretensions, and comes into the tavern announcing in a thick peasant brogue that the major is dead—"the late lamented auld liar and lunatic, Major Cornelius Melody, av his Majesty's Seventh Dragoons. . . . He didn't bother shooting himself, since it'd be a mad thing to waste a bullet on a corpse!" This is just theatrics; the part of the leering peasant is as much of a masquerade as the part of the major. But it allows the play to stop.

A play without hero or villain has a hard time stopping

or indeed going anywhere. The equivocal character of the central figure makes the action necessarily repetitious and irresolute, a seesaw of conflicting motives. Nothing for these people is *final*. The only play of the current group that definitively ends is *Deathwatch*, which is the only one with an uncompromising moral standard: Green Eyes has stayed aloof from the action, watching, like a *deus absconditus*, and then steps in to judge Lefranc as though he were Justice itself. There is nothing more to be said.

The Osborne play, his first, written in collaboration with Anthony Creighton, has already closed; public opinion did not like it. It was extraordinarily well acted, but this passed almost unnoticed, and why not? No one can tell the difference any more. Winsome Helen Hayes, that brave little body, was "hailed" for a performance in the O'Neill play that would have caused real uneasiness in a high school play; bent back, nodding, quavering head, tottering gait, copious winks, groans, and sly, rheumy grimaces left the impression that here was a child—plucky thing too—playing the part of a hobbling crone of forty or forty-five. It would be better to read the play than to be obliged to watch her, even though Eric Portman is sometimes very striking as Con Melody. The acting in the Genêt, done by young people, is quite passable.

Winter, 1958

Drapes

CURTAINS. KENNETH TYNAN. ATHENEUM. $7.95.

Is the title of this collection a pun ("It's curtains for me, pal")? Certainly, Tynan belongs to the school of wits who have been indentured to dramatic criticism: Beerbohm, Benchley, George Jean Nathan, Wolcott Gibbs. A turn-of-the-century example was the American humorist Eugene Field who said of a Claudius in *Hamlet*, "He plays the king as though somebody else were about to play the ace." Compare Tynan on Sir Ralph Richardson in *Macbeth*: ". . . a man long past feeling who had been stumping across the broad stage as if in need of a compass to find the exit." Or of an American "method" actor: ". . . he conforms to that modish acting technique, mistakenly associated with the teachings of Stanislavsky, whereby gesture precedes utterance by at least five seconds." Or—less drawling and japish—on Gielgud in modern dress: "The general aspect of a tight, smart, walking umbrella." The gift of characterizing a performance within a line or two is related to the gift of caricature; it is visual, like a cartoon. The written equivalent of caricature is surely parody, and Tynan, like Beerbohm, like Benchley, like Gibbs, is a facile parodist. He has very funny take-offs of Graham Greene, of Beckett, of Teutonic dialogue, of love scenes from English country-house

This review also appeared in *The Observer* of London.

comedy; the best is his parody of Faulkner's *Requiem for a Nun,* done in the style of the stage manager of Wilder's *Our Town:*

> "Well, folks, reckon that's about it. End of another day in the city of Jefferson, Yoknapatawpha County, Mississippi. Nothin' much happened. Couple of people got raped, couple more got their teeth kicked in, but way up there these faraway old stars are still doing their old cosmic criss-cross, and there ain't a thing we can do about it. Folks hereabouts get to bed early, those that can still walk. Down behind the morgue a few of the young people are roastin' a nigger over an open fire, but I guess every town has its night owls. . . . Movin' along toward dawn in our town. Pretty soon folks'll start up on that old diurnal round of sufferin' and expiatin' and spoutin' sentences two pages long. . . ."

This double play (the allusion is to baseball) catches two runners on base.

Parody in certain cases (like this one) may be the best criticism, as leaving the room may be the best means of ending an argument. But it is not criticism; it is a kind of quoting. No author can be parodied successfully who has not already committed self-parody. Parody begins where words, in the sense of rational discourse, fail the critic. Rational discourse is not Tynan's strong point. When, for example, he tries to make an intellectual demonstration of the weaknesses of MacLeish's *J. B.* and decides that these are due to the author's failure to take account of "Oriental philosophy," the reader would settle gladly for a simple parody: a Zen *J. B.* by MacLeish is too horribly easy to imagine—that is just the trouble. Like most of the humorists who have written about the theatre, Tynan is less a critic than a performer and mime in his own right; his reviews are excited performances. He can make you see and hear an actor, sometimes a whole play or rather its production; he can spot a defect or a virtue, but he cannot reason or analyze. It is interesting that in a long "probing" piece on Shaw he fails to mention his intelligence. Instead he discovers what he takes to be a telling fact about Shaw, a give-away: "as a public playwright he could not create an artist; Dubedat is a parasite, and Marchbanks is a hollow fraud. . . ." This evidently expects the reader-response "How terrible!" But what public playwright could "create an artist?" Sophocles, Shakespeare, Congreve, Molière, Wilde, John Osborne??? He suggests, sententiously, that Shaw was "scared to feel," yet there was a generous passion in Shaw that is absent from Tynan, who is most unconvincing when he is most in earnest, when he is writing valentines to Tennessee Williams, worshipping the Berliner Ensemble, exposing Ionesco ("as a serious thinker he is banal").

On his "positive" side, Tynan tends to write advertising copy. "This is an honest performance, true and watchful and ruthless." "The imposture is total and terrifying." "Peter Brook plants us firmly in Mexico." ". . . an artistic credo as stimulating as any in our time"—this of Arthur Miller's preface to *A View from the Bridge.* And of Miller and Tennessee Williams: "the finest two playwrights at present writing in English." "The exciting thing about Mr. Lawler is that he can also construct." This "quotable" manner of praising is sometimes like *Time* magazine, sometimes like *Mademoiselle:* "a select gaggle of alumni that includes Marlon Brando, Julie Harris, Eli Wallach, Marilyn Monroe . . ." He talks of "meaty" dialogue and refers to King Lear as "this huge flawed pyramid of a play." A "punchy" style of writing, packing in the metaphors, to advertise to the customers that it *is* writing.

At his best—on Sir Laurence Olivier, on Vivien Leigh —he is far, far better than these samples, but it is not a case of Homer nodding. In comparison with the average dramatic critic, he is a Angel, as Magwitch might say, but he will not bear comparison with Shaw, with Stark Young, with, today, Nicola Chiaromonte in Italy or

Francis Fergusson in America, though it is not fair, probably, to compare him with Fergusson, who is neither a journalist nor a wit—it is like comparing pears to green. The worst I can say of Tynan is that I thought better of him when I began this book than when I finished it. There is too much common coin here or protective coloration; you cannot tell the butterfly from the log. The profiles of and interviews with stars and celebrities—Bea Lillie, Gordon Craig, Tennessee Williams, Cagney, W. C. Fields —are like *New Yorker* profiles or Sunday feature stories: "cute" personality pieces, biography and physical impressions factory-woven with anecdotes. Taken at random from the Bea Lillie piece: "Offstage she leads a fairly intense social life and has arguably slept through more hours of daylight than of dark." The "fairly" and "arguably" are unarguable *New Yorker* profile. We learn in the same paragraph that her "last Christmas present to Noel Coward was a baby alligator." Cute? Such journalism can be produced by automation, with the reader's chuckles built in.

On the opposite façade of Tynan is a somewhat adenoidal spokesman-for-those-under-thirty—didactic and moralizing. His general ideas comprehend a preference for prose theatre over verse theatre, a preference, until recently, for foreign writers over English writers, a belief that the drama should show "respect for ordinary people," and a definition of drama (it shows human beings reduced by ineluctable process to a state of desperation). But these reiterated thoughts (and I cannot find any others except for the insistence that the theatre is a public place) are not so much ideas as crochets, like the crochets of an old person. His wit and humor, moreover, have the middle-aged quality of long-suffering—the classic henpecked humor of the drama reviewer wedded to a seat on the aisle. The drama reviewer in fact is an archetype of the human being reduced by ineluctable process to a state of desperation: a state well defined by Tynan in his remark about *Requiem for a Nun,* which he was see-

ing for the fourth time. "I begin to understand how
Francis Thompson felt when the Hound of Heaven picked
up his spoor." Very good.

Winter, 1962

My Confession

Every age has a keyhole to which its eye is pasted. Spicy court-memoirs, the lives of gallant ladies, recollections of an ex-nun, a monk's confession, an atheist's repentance, true-to-life accounts of prostitution and bastardy gave our ancestors a penny peep into the forbidden room. In our own day, this type of sensational fact-fiction is being produced largely by ex-Communists. Public curiosity shows an almost prurient avidity for the details of political defloration, and the memoirs of ex-Communists have an odd resemblance to the confessions of a white slave. Two shuddering climaxes, two rendezvous with destiny, form the poles between which these narratives vibrate: the first describes the occasion when the subject was seduced by Communism; the second shows him wresting himself from the demon embrace. Variations on the form are possible. Senator McCarthy, for example, in his book, *McCarthyism, the Fight for America,* uses a tense series of flashbacks to dramatize his encounter with Communism: the country lies passive in Communism's clasp; he is given a tryst with destiny in the lonely Arizona hills, where, surrounded by "real Americans without any synthetic sheen," he attains the decision that will send him down the long marble corridors to the Senate Caucus Room to bare the shameful commerce.

The diapason of choice plays, like movie music, round

today's apostle to the Gentiles: Whittaker Chambers on a park bench and, in a reprise, awake all night at a dark window, facing the void. These people, unlike ordinary beings, are shown the true course during a lightning storm of revelation, on the road to Damascus. And their decisions are lonely decisions, silhouetted against a background of public incomprehension and hostility.

I object. I have read the reminiscences of Mr. Chambers and Miss Bentley. I too have had a share in the political movements of our day, and my experience cries out against their experience. It is not the facts I balk at —I have never been an espionage agent—but the studio atmosphere of sublimity and purpose that enfolds the facts and the chief actor. When Whittaker Chambers is mounted on his tractor, or Elizabeth Bentley, alone, is meditating her decision in a white New England church, I have the sense that they are on location and that, at any moment, the director will call "Cut." It has never been like that for me; events have never waited, like extras, while I toiled to make up my mind between good and evil. In fact, I have never known these mental convulsions, which appear quite strange to me when I read about them, even when I do not question the author's sincerity.

Is it really so difficult to tell a good action from a bad one? I think one usually knows right away or a moment afterward, in a horrid flash of regret. And when one genuinely hesitates—or at least it is so in my case—it is never about anything of importance, but about perplexing trivial things, such as whether to have fish or meat for dinner, or whether to take the bus or subway to reach a certain destination, or whether to wear the beige or the green. The "great" decisions—those I can look back on pensively and say, "That was a turning-point"—have been made without my awareness. Too late to do anything about it, I discover that I have chosen. And this is particularly striking when the choice has been political or historic. For me, in fact, the mark of the historic is the nonchalance with which it picks up an individual and de-

posits him in a trend, like a house playfully moved by a
tornado. My own experience with Communism prompts
me to relate it, just because it had this inadvertence that
seems to me lacking in the true confessions of reformed
Communists. Like Stendhal's hero, who took part in
something confused and disarrayed and insignificant that
he later learned was the Battle of Waterloo, I joined the
anti-Communist movement without meaning to and only
found out afterward, through others, the meaning or
"name" assigned to what I had done. This occurred in
the late fall of 1936.

Three years before, I had graduated from college—
Vassar, the same college Elizabeth Bentley had gone to
—without having suffered any fracture of my political beliefs or moral frame. All through college, my official political philosophy was royalism; though I was not much
interested in politics, it irritated me to be told that "you
could not turn the clock back." But I did not see much
prospect for kingship in the United States (unless you
imported one, like the Swedes), and, *faute de mieux,* I
awarded my sympathies to the Democratic Party, which I
tried to look on as the party of the Southern patriciate.
At the same time, I had an aversion to Republicans—an
instinctive feeling that had been with me since I was a
child of eight pedaling my wagon up and down our
cement driveway and howling "Hurray for Cox" at the
Republican neighbors who passed by. I disliked businessmen and business attitudes partly, I think, because I came
from a professional (though Republican) family and had
picked up a disdain for businessmen as being beneath us,
in education and general culture. And the anti-Catholic
prejudice against Al Smith during the 1928 election,
the tinkling amusement at Mrs. Smith's vulgarity, democ-
ratized me a little in spite of myself: I was won by Smith's
plebeian charm, the big coarse nose, and rubbery politician's smile.

But this same distrust of uniformity made me shrink,
in 1932, from the sloppily dressed Socialist girls at col-

lege who paraded for Norman Thomas and tirelessly argued over "Cokes"; their eager fellowship and scrawled
placards and heavy personalities bored me—there was
something, to my mind, deeply athletic about this socialism. It was a kind of political hockey played by big, gaunt,
dyspeptic girls in pants. It startled me a little, therefore, to
learn that in an election poll taken of the faculty, several of my favorite teachers had voted for Thomas; in
them, the socialist faith appeared rather charming, I
decided—a gracious and attractive oddity, like the English Ovals they gave you when you came for tea. That
was the winter Hitler was coming to power and, hearing
of the anti-Jewish atrocities, I had a flurry of political
indignation. I wrote a prose-poem that dealt, in a mixed-
up way, with the Polish Corridor and the Jews. This
poem was so unlike me that I did not know whether to be
proud of it or ashamed of it when I saw it in a college
magazine. At this period, we were interested in surreal-
ism and automatic writing, and the poem had a certain
renown because it had come out of my interior without
much sense or order, just the way automatic writing was
supposed to do. But there my political development
stopped.

The depression was closer to home; in New York I
used to see apple-sellers on the street corners, and, now
and then, a bread line, but I had a very thin awareness of
mass poverty. The depression was too close to home to
awaken anything but curiosity and wonder—the feelings
of a child confronted with a death in the family. I was
conscious of the suicides of stockbrokers and businessmen, and of the fact that some of my friends had to go
on scholarships and had their dress allowances curtailed,
while their mothers gaily turned to doing their own cooking. To most of us at Vassar, I think, the depression
was chiefly an upper-class phenomenon.

My real interests were literary. In a paper for my
English Renaissance seminar, I noted a resemblance be-
tween the Elizabethan puritan pundits and the school of
Marxist criticism that was beginning to pontificate about

proletarian literature in the *New Masses*. I disliked the modern fanatics, cold, envious little clerics, equally with the insufferable and ridiculous Gabriel Harvey—Cambridge pedant and friend of Spenser—who tried to introduce the rules of Latin quantity into English verse and vilified a true poet who had died young, in squalor and misery. I really hated absolutism and officiousness of any kind (I preferred my kings martyred) and was pleased to be able to recognize a Zeal-of-the-Land-Busy in proletarian dress. And it was through a novel that I first learned, in my senior year, about the Sacco-Vanzetti case. The discovery that two innocent men had been executed only a few years back while I, oblivious, was in boarding school, gave me a disturbing shock. The case was still so near that I was tantalized by a feeling that it was not too late to do something—try still another avenue, if Governor Fuller and the Supreme Court obdurately would not be moved. An unrectified case of injustice has a terrible way of lingering, restlessly, in the social atmosphere like an unfinished equation. I went on to the Mooney case, which vexed not only my sense of equity but my sense of plausibility—how was it possible for the prosecution to lie so, in broad daylight, with the whole world watching?

When in May, 1933, however, before graduation, I went down to apply for a job at the old *New Republic* offices, I was not drawn there by the magazine's editorial policy—I hardly knew what it was—but because the book-review section seemed to me to possess a certain elegance and independence of thought that would be hospitable to a critical spirit like me. And I was badly taken aback when the book-review editor, to whom I had been shunted—there was no job—puffed his pipe and remarked that he would give me a review if I could show him that I was either a genius or starving. "I'm not starving," I said quickly; I knew I was not a genius and I was not pleased by the suggestion that I would be taking bread from other people's mouths. I did not think this a fair criterion and in a moment I said so. In reply, he put down his pipe, shrugged, reached out for the material I had brought with me, and half-promised, after an assaying glance, to send me a book. My notice finally appeared; it was not very good, but I did not know that and was elated. Soon I was reviewing novels and biographies for both the *New Republic* and the *Nation* and preening myself on the connection. Yet, whenever I entered the *New Republic's* waiting room, I was seized with a feeling of nervous guilt toward the shirtsleeved editors upstairs and their busy social conscience, and, above all, toward the shabby young men who were waiting too and who had, my bones told me, a better claim than I to the book I hoped to take away with me. They looked poor, pinched, scholarly, and supercilious, and I did not know which of these qualities made me, with my clicking high heels and fall "ensemble," seem more out of place.

I cannot remember the moment when I ceased to air my old royalist convictions and stuffed them away in an inner closet as you do a dress or an ornament that you perceive strikes the wrong note. It was probably at the time when I first became aware of Communists as a distinct entity. I had known about them, certainly, in college, but it was not until I came to New York that I began to have certain people, celebrities, pointed out to me as Communists and to turn my head to look at them, wonderingly. I had no wish to be one of them, but the fact that they were there—an unreckoned factor—made my own political opinions take on a protective coloration. This process was accelerated by my marriage—a week after graduation—to an actor and playwright who was in some ways very much like me. He was the son of a Minnesota normal school administrator who had been the scapegoat in an academic scandal that had turned him out of his job and reduced him, for a time, when my husband was nine or ten, to selling artificial limbs and encyclopedia sets from door to door. My husband still brooded over his father's misfortune, like Hamlet or a character in Ibsen, and this had given his nature a sardonic twist that inclined him to behave like a paradox —to follow the mode and despise it, live in a Beekman Place apartment while lacking the money to buy groceries, play bridge with society couples and poker with the stage electricians, dress in the English style and carry a walking stick while wearing a red necktie.

He was an odd-looking man, prematurely bald, with a tense, arresting figure, a broken nose, a Standard English accent, and wry, circumflexed eyebrows. There was something about him both baleful and quizzical; whenever he stepped on the stage he had the ironic air of a symbol. This curious appearance of his disqualified him for most Broadway roles; he was too young for character parts and too bald for juveniles. Yet just this disturbing ambiguity—a Communist painter friend did a drawing of him that brought out a resemblance to Lenin—suited the portentous and equivocal atmosphere of left-wing drama. He smiled dryly at Marxist terminology, but there was social anger in him. During the years we were married, the only work he found was in productions of "social" significance. He played for the Theatre Union in *The Sailors of Cattaro,* about a mutiny in the Austrian fleet, and in *Black Pit,* about coal miners; the following year, he was in *Winterset* and Archibald MacLeish's *Panic*—the part of a blind man in both cases. He wrote revue sketches and unproduced plays, in a mocking, despairing, but none the less radical vein; he directed the book of a musical called *Americana* that featured the song, "Brother, Can You Spare a Dime?" I suppose there was something in him of both the victim and the leader, an undertone of totalitarianism; he was very much interested in the mythic qualities of leadership and talked briskly about a Farmer-Labor party in his stage English accent. Notions of the superman and the genius flickered across his thoughts. But this led him, as it happened, away from politics, into sheer personal vitalism, and it was only in plays that he entered "at the head of a mob." In personal life he was very winning, but that is beside the point here.

The point is that we both, through our professional

connections, began to take part in a left-wing life, to which we felt superior, which we laughed at, but which nevertheless was influencing us without our being aware of it. If the composition of the body changes every seven years, the composition of our minds during the seven years changed, so that though our thoughts looked the same to us, inside we had been altered, like an old car which has had part after part replaced in it under the hood.

We wore our rue with a difference; we should never have considered joining the Communist Party. We were not even fellow-travelers; we did not sign petitions or join "front" groups. We were not fools, after all, and were no more deceived by the League against War and Fascism, say, than by a Chinatown bus with a carload of shills aboard. It was part of our metropolitan sophistication to know the truth about Communist fronts. We accepted the need for social reform, but we declined to draw the "logical" inference that the Communists wanted us to draw from this. We argued with the comrades backstage in the dressing rooms and at literary cocktail parties; I was attacked by a writer in the *New Masses*. We knew about Lovestoneites and Trotskyites, even while we were ignorant of the labor theory of value, the law of uneven development, the theory of permanent revolution *vs.* socialism in one country, and so on. "Lovestone is a Lovestoneite!" John wrote in wax on his dressing-room mirror, and on his door in the old Civic Repertory he put up a sign: "Through these portals pass some of the most beautiful tractors in the Ukraine."

The comrades shrugged and laughed, a little unwillingly. They knew we were not hostile but merely unserious, politically. The comrades who knew us best used to assure us that our sophistication was just an armor; underneath, we must care for the same things they did. They were mistaken, I am afraid. Speaking for myself, I cannot remember a single broad altruistic emotion visiting me during that period—the kind of emotion the simpler comrades, with their shining eyes and exalted faces, seemed to have in copious secretion. And yet it was true: we were not hostile. We marched in May Day parades, just for the fun of it, and sang, "Hold the Fort, for We Are Coming," and *"Bandiera Rosa,"* and "The Internationale," though we always bellowed "The *Socialist* International shall be the human race," instead of "The International Soviet," to pique the Communists in our squad. We took part in evening clothes in a consumers' walkout at the Waldorf to support a waiters' strike—the Communists had nothing to do with this—and we grew very excited (we did have negative feelings) when another young literary independent was arrested and booked. During a strike at a department store, John joined the sympathetic picketing and saw two of his fellow actors carried off in the Black Maria; they missed a matinee and set off a controversy about what was the *first* responsibility of a Communist playing in a proletarian drama. We went once or twice to a class for actors in Marxism, just to see what was up; we went to a debate on Freud and/or Marx, to a debate on the execution of the hundred and four White Guards following Kirov's assassination.

Most ex-Communists nowadays, when they write their autobiographies or testify before Congressional committees, are at pains to point out that their actions were very, very bad and their motives very, very good. I would say the reverse of myself, though without the intensives. I see no reason to disavow my actions, which were perfectly all right, but my motives give me a little embarrassment, and just because I cannot disavow them: that fevered, contentious, trivial show-off in the May Day parade is still recognizably me.

We went to dances at Webster Hall and took our uptown friends. We went to parties to raise money for the sharecroppers, for the Theatre Union, for the *New Masses*. These parties generally took place in a borrowed apartment, often a sculptor's or commercial artist's studio; you paid for your drinks, which were dispensed at a long, wet table; the liquor was dreadful; the glasses were small, and there was never enough ice. Long-haired men in turtle-necked sweaters marched into the room in processions and threw their overcoats on the floor, against the wall, and sat on them; they were only artists and bit-actors, but they gave these affairs a look of gangsterish menace, as if the room were guarded by the goons of the future. On couches with wrinkled slipcovers, little spiky-haired girls, like spiders, dressed in peasant blouses and carapaced with Mexican jewelry, made voracious passes at baby-faced juveniles; it was said that they "did it for the Party," as a recruiting effort. Vague, soft-faced old women with dust mops of whitish hair wandered benevolently about seeking a listener; on a sofa against a wall, like a deity, sat a bearded scion of an old Boston family, stiff as a post. All of us, generally, became very drunk; the atmosphere was horribly sordid, with cigarette burns on tables, spilled drinks, ashes everywhere, people passed out on the bed with the coats or necking, you could not be sure which. Nobody cared what happened because there was no host or hostess. The fact that a moneyed person had been simple enough to lend the apartment seemed to make the guests want to desecrate it, to show that they were exercising not a privilege but a right.

Obviously, I must have hated these parties, but I went to them, partly because I was ashamed of my own squeamishness, and partly because I had a curiosity about the Communist men I used to see there, not the actors or writers, but the higher-ups, impresarios and theoreticians —dark, smooth-haired owls with large white lugubrious faces and glasses. These were the spiritual directors of the Communist cultural celebrities and they moved about at these parties like so many monks or abbés in a worldly salon. I had always liked to argue with the clergy, and I used to argue with these men, who had the air, as they stood with folded arms, of listening not to a disagreement but to a confession. Whenever I became tight, I would bring up (oh, *vino veritas*) the Czar and his family. I did not see why they all had had to be killed—the Czar himself, yes, perhaps, and the Czarina, but not the young girls and the children. I knew the answer, of course (the young Czarevitch or one of his sisters might have served as a rallying point for the counter-revolutionary forces), but still I gazed hopefully into these docents' faces, seeking a trace of scruple or compassion. But I saw only a marmoreal astuteness. The question was of bourgeois origin, they said with finality.

The next morning I was always bitterly ashamed. I had let these omniscient men see the real me underneath, and the other me squirmed and gritted her teeth and muttered, Never, never, *never* again. And yet they had not convinced me—there was the paradox. The superiority I felt to the Communists I knew had, for me at any rate, good grounding; it was based on their lack of humor, their fanaticism, and the slow drip of cant that thickened their utterance like a nasal catarrh. *And yet* I was tremendously impressed by them. They made me feel petty and shallow; they had, shall I say, a daily ugliness in their life that made my pretty life tawdry. I think all of us who moved in that ambience must have felt something of the kind, even while we laughed at them. When John and I, for instance, would say of a certain actor, "He is a Party member," our voices always contained a note of respect. This respect might be mixed with pity, as when we saw some blue-eyed young profile, fresh from his fraternity and his C average, join up because a sleazy girl had persuaded him. The literary Communists I sincerely despised because I was able to judge the quality of the work they published and see their dishonesty and contradictions; even so, when I beheld them in person, at a Webster Hall dance, I was troubled and felt perhaps I had wronged them—perhaps there was something in them that my vision could not perceive, as some eyes cannot perceive color.

People sometimes say that they envied the Communists because they were so "sure." In my case, this was not exactly it; I was sure, too, intellectually speaking, as far as I went. That is, I had a clear mind and was reasonably honest, while many of the Communists I knew were pathetically fogged up. In any case, my soul was not particularly hot for certainties.

And yet in another way I did envy the Communists, or, to be more accurate, wonder whether I ought to envy them. I could not, I saw, be a Communist because I was not "made that way." Hence, to be a Communist was to possess a sort of privilege. And this privilege, like all privileges, appeared to be a source of power. Any form of idiocy or aberration can confer this distinction on its owner, at least in our age, which aspires to a "total" experience; in the thirties it was the Communists who seemed fearsomely to be the happy few, not because they had peace or certitude but because they were a mutation —a mutation that threatened, in the words of their own anthem, to become the human race.

There was something arcane in every Communist, and the larger this area was the more we respected him. That was why the literary Communists, who operated in the open, doing the hatchet work on artists' reputations, were held in such relatively low esteem. An underground worker rated highest with us; next were the theoreticians and oracles; next were the activists, who mostly worked, we heard, on the waterfront. Last came the rank and file, whose work consisted of making speeches, distributing leaflets, attending Party and faction meetings, joining front organizations, marching in parades and demonstrations. These people we dismissed as uninteresting not so much because their work was routine but because the greater part of it was visible. In the same way, among individual comrades, we looked up to those who were close-lipped and stern about their beliefs and we disparaged the more voluble members—the forensic little actors who tried to harangue us in the dressing rooms. The idea of a double life was what impressed us: the more talkative comrades seemed to have only one life, like us; but even they, we had to remind ourselves, had a secret annex to their personality, which was signified by their Party name. It is hard not to respect somebody who has an alias.

Of fellow-travelers, we had a very low opinion. People who were not willing to "go the whole way" filled us with impatient disdain. The only fellow-travelers who merited our notice were those of whom it was said: the Party prefers that they remain on the outside. I think some fellow-travelers circulated such stories about themselves deliberately, in order to appear more interesting. There was another type of fellow-traveler who let it be known that they stayed out of the Party because of some tiny doctrinal difference with Marxism. This tiny difference magnified them enormously in their own eyes and allowed them to bear gladly the accusation of cowardice. I knew one such person very well—a spruce, ingratiating swain, the heir to a large fortune—and I think it was not cowardice but a kind of pietistic vanity. He felt he cut more of a figure if he seemed to be doing the Party's dirty work gratuitously, without compulsion, like an oblate.

In making these distinctions (which were the very distinctions the Party made), I had no idea, of course, that I was allowing myself to be influenced by the Party in the field where I was most open to suasion—the field of social snobbery. Yet in fact I was being deterred from forming any political opinions of my own, lest I find I was that despised article, a "mere" socialist or watery liberal, in the same way that a young snob coming to college and seeing who the "right" people are will strive to make no friends rather than be caught with the wrong ones.

For me, the Communist Party was *the* party, and even though I did not join it, I prided myself on knowing that it was the pinnacle. It is only now that I see the social component in my attitude. At the time, I simply supposed that I was being clear-sighted and logical. I used to do research and typing for a disgruntled middle-aged man who was a freak for that day—an anti-Communist Marxist—and I was bewildered by his anti-Party bias. While we were drinking hot tea, Russian style, from glasses during the intervals of our work, I would try to show him his mistake. "Don't you think it's rather futile," I expostulated, "to criticize the Party the way you do, from the outside? After all, it's the *only* working-class Party, and if *I* were a Marxist I would join it and try to reform it." Snorting, he would raise his small deep-set blue eyes and stare at me and then try patiently to show me that there was no democracy in the Party. I listened disbelievingly. It seemed to me that it would just be a question of converting first one comrade and then another to your point of view till gradually you had achieved a majority. And when my employer assured me that they would throw you out if you tried that, my twenty-three-year-old wisdom cocked an eyebrow. I thought I knew what was the trouble: he was a pathologically lazy man and his growling criticisms of the Party were simply a form of malingering, like the aches and pains he used to manufacture to avoid working on an article. A real revolutionary who was not afraid of exertion would get into the Party and fight.

The curious idea that being critical of the Party was a compelling reason for joining it must have been in the air, for the same argument was brought to bear on me in the summer of 1936—the summer my husband and I separated and that I came closest to the gravitational pull of the Communist world. Just before I went off to Reno, there was a week in June when I stayed in Southampton with the young man I was planning to marry and a little Communist organizer in an old summer house furnished with rattan and wicker and Chinese matting and mother-of-pearl and paper fans. We had come there for a purpose. The little organizer had just been assigned a car—a battered old Ford roadster that had been turned over to the Party for the use of some poor organizer; it may have been the very car that figured in the Hiss case. My fiancé, who had known him for years, perhaps from the peace movement, was going to teach him to drive. We were all at a pause in our lives. The following week our friend was supposed to take the car to California and do propaganda work among the migrant fruit-pickers; I was to go to Reno; my fiancé, a vivacious young bachelor, was to conquer his habits of idleness and buckle down to a serious job.

Those seven days, therefore, had a special, still quality, like the days of a novena you make in your childhood; a part of each of them was set aside for the Party's task. It was early in June; the musty house that belonged to my fiancé's parents still had the winter-smell of mice and old wood and rust and mildew. The summer colony had not yet arrived; the red flag, meaning that it was dangerous to swim, flew daily on the beach; the roads were nearly empty. Every afternoon we would take the old car, canvas flapping, to a deserted stretch of straight road in the dunes, where the neophyte could take the wheel.

He was a large-browed, dwarfish man in his late thirties, with a deep widow's peak, a bristly short mustache, and a furry western accent—rather simple, open-natured, and cheerful, the sort of person who might have been a small-town salesman or itinerant newspaperman. There was an energetic, hopeful innocence about him that was not confined to his political convictions—he could *not* learn to drive. Every day the same thing happened; he would settle his frail yet stocky figure trustingly in the driver's seat, grip the wheel, step on the starter, and lose control of the car, which would shoot ahead in first or backward in reverse for a few perilous feet till my fiancé turned off the ignition; Ansel always mistook the gas for the brake and forgot to steer while he was shifting gears.

It was clear that he would never be able to pass the driver's test at the county seat. In the evenings, to make up to him for his oncoming disappointment (we smiled when he said he could start without a license), we encouraged him to talk about the Party and tried to take an intelligent interest. We would sit by the lamp and drink and ask questions, while he smoked his short pipe and from time to time took a long draught from his highball, like a man alone musing in a chair.

And finally one night, in the semi-dark, he knocked out his pipe and said to me: "You're very critical of the Party. Why don't you join it?" A thrill went through me, but I laughed, as when somebody has proposed to you and you are not sure whether they are serious. "I don't think I'd

make very good material." "You're wrong," he said gravely. "You're just the kind of person the Party needs. You're
young and idealistic and independent." I broke in: "I
thought independence was just what the Party didn't
want." "The Party needs criticism," he said. "But it needs
it from the inside. If people like you who agree with its
main objectives would come in and criticize, we wouldn't
be so narrow and sectarian." "You admit the Party is
narrow?" exclaimed my fiancé. "Sure, I admit it," said
Ansel, grinning. "But it's partly the fault of people like
Mary who won't come in and broaden us." And he con-
fided that he himself made many of the same criticisms I
did, but he made them from within the Party, and so could
get himself listened to. "The big problem of the American Party," said Ansel, puffing at his pipe, "is the smallness of the membership. People say we're ruled from Moscow; I've never seen any sign of it. But let's suppose it's
true, for the sake of argument. This just means that the
American Party isn't big enough yet to stand on its own
feet. A big, indigenous party couldn't be ruled from Moscow. The will of the members would have to rule it, just
as their dues and contributions would support it." "That's
where I come in, I suppose?" I said, teasing. "That's where
you come in," he calmly agreed. He turned to my fiancé.
"Not you," he said. "You won't have the time to give to
it. But for Mary I think it would be an interesting experiment."

An interesting experiment . . . I let the thought wander
through my mind. The subject recurred several times, by
the lamplight, though with no particular urgency. Ansel,
I thought (and still think), was speaking sincerely and
partly in my own interest, almost as a spectator, as if he
would be diverted to see how I worked out in the Party.
All this gave me quite a new sense of Communism and of
myself too; I had never looked upon my character in such
a favorable light. And as a beneficiary of Ansel's charity,
I felt somewhat ashamed of the very doubt it raised: the
suspicion that he might be blind to the real facts of inner
Party life. I could admire where I could not follow, and,

studying Ansel, I decided that I admired the Communists
and would probably be one, if I were the person he
thought me. Which I was afraid I was not. For me, such
a wry conclusion is always uplifting, and I had the feeling that I mounted in understanding when Sunday morning came and I watched Ansel pack his sturdy suitcase
and his briefcase full of leaflets into the old roadster. He
had never yet driven more than a few yards by himself,
and we stood on the front steps to await what was going
to happen: he would not be able to get out of the driveway, and we would have to put him on the train and return the car to the Party when we came back to New
York. As we watched, the car began to move; it picked up
speed and grated into second, holding to the middle of the
road as it turned out of the driveway. It hesitated and
went into third: Ansel was driving! Through the back
window we saw his figure hunched over the wheel; the
road dipped and he vanished. We had witnessed a miracle,
and we turned back into the house, frightened. All day
we sat waiting for the call that would tell us there had
been an accident, but the day passed without a sound,
and by nightfall we accepted the phenomenon and pic-
tured the little car on the highway, traveling steadily west
in one indefatigable thrust, not daring to stop for gas or
refreshment, lest the will of the driver falter.

This parting glimpse of Ansel through the car's back
window was, as it turned out, ultimate. Politically speaking, we reached a watershed that summer. The first Moscow trial took place in August. I knew nothing of this event
because I was in Reno and did not see the New York
papers. Nor did I know that the Party line had veered to
the right and that all the fellow-travelers would be voting,
not for Browder as I was now prepared to do (if only I
remembered to register), but for Roosevelt. Isolated from
these developments in the mountain altitudes, I was blos-
soming, like a lone winter rose overlooked by the frost,
into a revolutionary thinker of the pure, uncompromising
strain. The detached particles of the past three years'

and the *Liberator*. Their names were whispered to me and
I nodded; this seemed to be a commemorative occasion,
and the young men hovered in groups around the old
men, as if to catch a word for posterity. On the outskirts
of certain groups I noticed a few poorly dressed young
men, bolder spirits, nervously flexing their lips, framing
sentences that would propel them into the conversational
center, like actors with a single line to speak.

The solemnity of these proceedings made me feel terribly ill at ease. It was some time before I became aware
that it was not just me who was nervous: the whole room
was under a constraint. Some groups were avoiding other
groups, and now and then an arrow of sarcasm would
wing like a sniper's bullet from one conversation to another.

I was standing, rather bleakly, by the refreshment table, when a question was thrust at me: did I think Trotsky was entitled to a hearing? It was a novelist friend of
mine, dimple-faced, shaggy-headed, earnest, with a whole
train of people, like a deputation, behind him. Trotsky?
I glanced for help at a sour little man I had been talking
with, but he merely shrugged. My friend made a beckon-
ing gesture and a circle closed in. What had Trotsky
done? Alas, I had to ask. A tumult of voices proffered
explanations. My friend raised a hand for silence. Leaning on the table, he supplied the background, speaking
very slowly, in his dragging, disconsolate voice, like a
schoolteacher wearied of his subject. Trotsky, it appeared,
had been accused of fostering a counter-revolutionary plot
in the Soviet Union—organizing terrorist centers and con-
spiring with the Gestapo to murder the Soviet leaders.
Sixteen old Bolsheviks had confessed and implicated him.
It had been in the press since August.

I blushed; everybody seemed to be looking at me
strangely. I made a violent effort to take in what had been
said. The enormity of the charge dazed me, and I supposed that some sort of poll was being taken and that I
was being asked to pronounce on whether Trotsky was
guilty or innocent. I could tell from my friend's low, even,

melancholy tone that he regarded the charges as derisory. "What do you want me to say?" I protested. "I don't know anything about it." "Trotsky denies the charges," patiently intoned my friend. "He declares it's a GPU fabrication. Do you think he's entitled to a hearing?" My mind cleared. "Why, of course." I laughed—were there people who would say that Trotsky was *not* entitled to a hearing? But my friend's voice tolled a rebuke to this levity. "She says Trotsky is entitled to his day in court."

The sour little man beside me made a peculiar, sucking noise. "You disagree?" I demanded, wonderingly. "I'm smart," he retorted. "I don't let anybody ask me. You notice, he doesn't ask me?" "Shut up, George," said my novelist friend impatiently. "I'm asking *her*. One thing more, Mary," he continued gravely. "Do you believe that Trotsky should have the right of asylum?" The right of asylum! I looked for someone to share my amusement— were we in ancient Greece or the Middle Ages? I was sure the U.S. government would be delighted to harbor such a distinguished foreigner. But nobody smiled back. Everybody watched dispassionately, as for form's sake I assented to the phrasing: yes, Trotsky, in my opinion, was entitled to the right of asylum.

I went home with the serene feeling that all these people were slightly crazy. *Right of asylum, his day in court!* —in a few hours I had forgotten the whole thing.

Four days later I tore open an envelope addressed to me by something that called itself "Committee for the Defense of Leon Trotsky," and idly scanned the contents. "We demand for Leon Trotsky the right of a fair hearing and the right of asylum." Who were these demanders, I wondered, and, glancing down the letterhead, I discovered my own name. I sat down on my unmade studio couch, shaking. How dared they help themselves to my signature? This was the kind of thing the Communists were always being accused of pulling; apparently, Trotsky's admirers had gone to the same school. I had paid so little heed to the incident at the party that a connection was slow to establish itself. Reading over the list of signers, I recognized "names" that had been present there and remembered my novelist friend going from person to person, methodically polling. . . .

How were they feeling, I wondered, when they opened their mail this morning? My own feelings were crisp. In two minutes I had decided to withdraw my name and write a note of protest. Trotsky had a right to a hearing, but I had a right to my signature. For even if there had been a legitimate misunderstanding (it occurred to me that perhaps I had been the only person there not to see the import of my answers), nothing I had said committed me to Trotsky's *defense*.

The "decision" was made, but according to my habit I procrastinated. The severe letter I proposed to write got put off till the next day and then the next. Probably I was not eager to offend somebody who had been a good friend to me. Nevertheless, the letter would undoubtedly have been written, had I been left to myself. But within the next forty-eight hours the phone calls began. People whom I had not seen for months or whom I knew very slightly telephoned to advise me to get off the newly formed Committee. These calls were not precisely threatening. Indeed, the caller often sounded terribly weak and awkward, as if he did not like the mission he had been assigned. But they were peculiar. For one thing, they usually came after nightfall and sometimes quite late, when I was already in bed. Another thing, there was no real effort at persuasion: the caller stated his purpose in standardized phrases, usually plaintive in tone (the Committee was the tool of reaction, and all liberal people should dissociate themselves from its activities, which were an unwarranted intervention in the domestic affairs of the Soviet Union), and then hung up, almost immediately, before I had a proper chance to answer. Odd too— the voices were not those of my Communist friends but of the merest acquaintances. These people who admonished me to "think about it" were not people whose individual opinions could have had any weight with me. And when

I did think about it, this very fact took on an ominous and yet to me absurd character: I was not being appealed to personally but impersonally warned.

Behind these phone calls there was a sense of the Party wheeling its forces into would-be disciplined formations, like a fleet or an army maneuvering. This, I later found, was true: a systematic telephone campaign was going on to dislodge members from the Committee. The phone calls generally came after dark and sometimes (especially when the recipient was elderly) in the small hours of the morning. The more prominent signers got anonymous messages and threats.

And in the morning papers and the columns of the liberal magazines I saw the results. During the first week, name after name fell off the Committee's letterhead. Prominent liberals and literary figures issued statements deploring their mistake. And a number of people protested that their names had been used without permission. . . .

There, but for the grace of God, went I, I whispered, awestruck, to myself, hugging my guilty knowledge. Only Heaven—I plainly saw—by making me dilatory had preserved me from joining this sorry band. Here was the occasion when I should have been wrestling with my conscience or standing, floodlit, at the crossroads of choice. But in fact I was only aware that I had had a providential escape. I had been saved from having to decide about the Committee; *I* did not decide it—the Communists with their pressure tactics took the matter out of my hands. We all have an instinct that makes us side with the weak, if we do not stop to reason about it, the instinct that makes a householder shield a wounded fugitive without first conducting an inquiry into the rights and wrongs of his case. Such "decisions" are simple reflexes; they do not require courage; if they did, there would be fewer of them. When I saw what was happening, I rebounded to the defense of the Committee without a single hesitation—it was nobody's business, I felt, how I happened to be on it, and if anybody had asked me, I should have lied without a scruple.

Of course, I did not foresee the far-reaching consequences of my act—how it would change my life. I had no notion that I was now an anti-Communist, where before I had been either indifferent or pro-Communist. I did, however, soon recognize that I was in a rather awkward predicament—not a moral quandary but a social one. I knew nothing about the cause I had espoused; I had never read a word of Lenin or Trotsky, nothing of Marx but the *Communist Manifesto,* nothing of Soviet history; the very names of the old Bolsheviks who had confessed were strange and almost barbarous in my ears. As for Trotsky, the only thing that made me think that he might be innocent was the odd behavior of the Communists and the fellow-traveling liberals, who seemed to be infuriated at the idea of a free inquiry. All around me, in the fashionable Stalinist circles I was now frequenting, I began to meet with suppressed excitement and just-withheld disapproval. Jeweled lady-authors turned white and shook their bracelets angrily when I came into a soirée; rising young men in publishing or advertising tightened their neckties dubiously when I urged them to examine the case for themselves; out dancing in a night club, tall, collegiate young Party members would press me to their shirt-bosoms and tell me not to be silly, honey.

And since I seemed to meet more Stalinists every day, I saw that I was going to have to get some arguments with which to defend myself. It was not enough, apparently, to say you were for a fair hearing; you had to rebut the entire case of the prosecution to get anybody to incline an ear in your direction. I began to read, headlong, the literature on the case—the pamphlets issued by Trotsky's adherents, the verbatim report of the second trial published by the Soviet Union, the "bourgeois" press, the Communist press, the radical press. To my astonishment (for I had scarcely dared think it), the trials did indeed seem to be a monstrous frame-up. The defendant, Pyatakov, flew to Oslo to "conspire" with Trotsky during a winter when, according to the authorities, no

planes landed at the Oslo airfield; the defendant, Holtz-
mann, met Trotsky's son, Sedov, in 1936, at the Hotel
Bristol in Copenhagen, which had burned down in 1912;
the witness, Romm, met Trotsky in Paris at a time when
numerous depositions testified that he had been in Royan,
among clouds of witnesses, or on the way there from the
south of France.

These were only the most glaring discrepancies—the
ones that got in the newspapers. Everywhere you touched
the case something crumbled. The carelessness of the
case's manufacture was to me its most terrifying aspect;
the slovenly disregard for credibility defied credence, in
its turn. How did they dare? I think I was more shaken
by finding that I was on the right side than I would have
been the other way round. And yet, except for a very
few people, nobody seemed to mind whether the Hotel
Bristol had burned down or not, whether a real plane
had landed, whether Trotsky's life and writings were con-
gruent with the picture given of him in the trials. When
confronted with the facts of the case, people's minds
sheered off from it like jelly from a spoon.

Anybody who has ever tried to rectify an injustice or
set a record straight comes to feel that he is going mad.
And from a social point of view, he *is* crazy, for he is
trying to undo something that is finished, to unravel the
social fabric. That is why my liberal friends looked so
grave and solemn when I would press them to come to
a meeting and listen to a presentation of the facts—for
them this was a Decison, too awful to be considered lightly.
The Moscow trials were a historical fact and those of
us who tried to undo them were uneasily felt to be crack-
pots, who were trying to turn the clock back. And of
course the less we were listened to, the more insistent
and earnest we became, even while we realized we were
doing our cause harm. It is impossible to take a moderate
tone under such conditions. If I admitted, though, to being
a little bit hipped on the subject of Trotsky, I could sometimes gain an indulgent if flickering attention—the kind of
attention that stipulates, "She's a bit off but let's hear her

story." And now and then, by sheer chance, one of my hearers would be arrested by some stray point in my narrative; the disparaging smile would slowly fade from his features, leaving a look of blank consternation. He would go off and investigate for himself, and in a few days, when we met again, he would be a crackpot too.

Most of us who became anti-Communists at the time of the trials were drawn in, like me, by accident and almost unwillingly. Looking back, as on a love affair, a man could say that if he had not had lunch in a certain restaurant on a certain day, he might not have been led to ponder the facts of the Moscow trials. Or not then at any rate. And had he pondered them at a later date, other considerations would have entered and his conversion would have had a different style. On the whole, those of us who became anti-Communists during that year, 1936-37, have remained liberals—a thing that is less true of people of our generation who were converted earlier or later. A certain doubt of orthodoxy and independence of mass opinion was riveted into our anti-Communism by the heat of that period. As soon as I make this statement, exceptions leap into my mind, but I think as a generalization it will stand. Those who became anti-Communist earlier fell into two classes: the experts and those to whom any socialist ideal was repugnant. Those whose eyes were opened later, by the Nazi-Soviet pact, or still later, by God knows what, were left bruised and full of self-hatred or self-commiseration, because they had palliated so much and truckled to a power-center; to them, Communism's chief sin seems to be that it deceived *them,* and their public atonement takes on both a vindicating and a vindictive character.

We were luckier. Our anti-Communism came to us neither as the fruit of a special wisdom nor as a humiliating awakening from a prolonged deception, but as a natural event, the product of chance and propinquity. One thing followed another, and the will had little to say about it. For my part, during that year, I realized, with a certain wistfulness, that it was too late for me to become any kind of Marxist. Marxism, I saw, from the learned young men I listened to at Committee meetings, was something you had to take up young, like ballet dancing.

So, I did not try to be a Marxist or a Trotskyite, though for the first time I read a little in the Marxist canon. But I got the name of being a Trotskyite, which meant, in the end, that I saw less of the conventional Stalinists I had been mingling with and less of conventional people generally. (My definition of a conventional person was quite broad: it included anyone who could hear of the Moscow trials and maintain an unruffled serenity.) This, then, was a break or a rupture, not very noticeable at first, that gradually widened and widened, without any conscious effort on my part, sometimes to my regret. This estrangement was not marked by any definite stages; it was a matter of tiny choices. Shortly after the Moscow trials, for instance, I changed from the *Herald Tribune* to the *Times*; soon I had stopped doing crossword puzzles, playing bridge, reading detective stories and popular novels. I did not "give up" these things; they departed from me, as it were, on tiptoe, seeing that my thoughts were elsewhere.

To change from the *Herald Tribune* to the *Times*, is not, I am aware, as serious a step as breaking with international Communism when you have been its agent; and it occurs to me that Mr. Chambers and Miss Bentley might well protest the comparison, pointing out that they were profoundly dedicated people, while I was a mere trifler, that their decisions partook of the sublime, where mine descended to the ridiculous—as Mr. Chambers says, he was ready to give his life for his beliefs. Fortunately (though I could argue the point, for we all give our lives for our beliefs, piecemeal or whole), I have a surprise witness to call for my side, who did literally die for his political views.

I am referring to Trotsky, the small, frail, pertinacious old man who wore whiskers, wrinkles, glasses, shock of grizzled hair, like a gleeful disguise for the erect young student, the dangerous revolutionary within him. Nothing could be more alien to the convulsed and tormented moonscapes of the true confessions of ex-Communists than Trotsky's populous, matter-of-fact recollections set out in *My Life*. I have just been rereading this volume, and though I no longer subscribe to its views, which have certainly an authoritarian and doctrinaire cast that troubles me today, nevertheless I experience a sense of recognition here that I cannot find in the pages of our own repentant "revolutionaries." The old man remained unregenerate; he never admitted that he had sinned. That is probably why nobody seems to care for, or feel apologetic to, his memory. It is an interesting point— and relevant, I think, to my story—that many people today actually have the impression that Trotsky died a natural death.

In a certain sense, this is perfectly true. I do not mean that he lived by violence and therefore might reasonably be expected to die by violence. He was a man of words primarily, a pamphleteer and orator. He was armed, as he said, with a pen and peppered his enemies with a fusillade of articles. Hear the concluding passages of his autobiography: "Since my exile, I have more than once read musings in the newspapers on the subject of the 'tragedy' that has befallen me. I know no *personal* tragedy. I know the change of two chapters of revolution. One American paper which published an article of mine accompanied it with a profound note to the effect that in spite of the blows the author had suffered, he had, as evidenced by his article, preserved his clarity of reason. I can only express my astonishment at the Philistine attempt to establish a connection between the power of reasoning and a government post, between mental balance and the present situation. I do not know, and never have known, of any such connection. In prison, with a book or pen in my hand, I experienced the same sense of deep satisfaction that I did at mass-meetings of the revolution. I felt the mechanics of power as an inescapable burden, rather than as a spiritual satisfaction."

This was not a man of violence. Nevertheless, one can say that he died a natural death—a death that was in keeping with the open manner of his life. There was nothing arcane in Trotsky; that was his charm. Like an ordinary person he was hospitably open to hazard and accident. In his autobiography, he cannot date the moment when he became a socialist.

One factor in his losing out in the power-struggle at the time of Lenin's death was his delay in getting the telegram that should have called him home from the Caucasus, where he was convalescent, to appear at Lenin's funeral—*had* he got the telegram, the outcome perhaps would have been different. Or again, perhaps not. It may be that the whims of chance are really the importunities of design. But if there is a Design, it aims, in real lives, like the reader's or mine or Trotsky's, to look natural and fortuitous; that is how it gets us into its web.

Trotsky himself, looking at his life in retrospect, was struck, as most of us are on such occasions, by the role chance had played in it. He tells how one day, during Lenin's last illness, he went duck-shooting with an old hunter in a canoe on the River Dubna, walked through a bog in felt boots—only a hundred steps—and contracted influenza. This was the reason he was ordered to Sukhu for the cure, missed Lenin's funeral, and had to stay in bed during the struggle for primacy that raged that autumn and winter. "I cannot help noting," he says, "how obligingly the accidental helps the historical law. Broadly speaking, the entire historical process is a refraction of historical law through the accidental. In the language of biology, one might say that the historical law is realized through the natural selection of accidents." And with a touch of quizzical gaiety he sums up the problem as a Marxian: "One can foresee the consequences of a revolution or a war, but it is impossible to foresee the consequences of an autumn shooting-trip for wild ducks." This shrug before the unforeseen implies an acceptance of consequences that is a far cry from penance and prophecy. Such, it concedes, is life. *Bravo,* old sport, I say, even though the hall is empty.

Fall, 1953

Tyranny of the Orgasm

Statistics compiled by Dr. Kinsey of the University of Indiana give the text for today's sermon preached by a journalist and a woman psychiatrist to the women of America. Using the Gallup Poll method, Dr. Kinsey discovered that from 50 to 85 per cent of American women college graduates had never experienced an orgasm. High school graduates had a better record; less than 20 per cent reported the same deficiency. The percentage continued to decline as schooling was less intensive, and among uneducated Negro women the incidence of orgasm was nearly 100 per cent. If frigidity is to be viewed as a national scandal on a par with political corruption and inadequate housing, the remedy at least seems obvious. The mother of little girls has only to present Dr. Kinsey's figures to the truant officer. Mr. Ferdinand Lundberg and Dr. Marynia F. Farnham, however, disclaiming such hasty inferences, arrive at the same result by a more devious route. Their book is an adjuration to American women to return to the home and leave men's pursuits to men. Their itinerary to his conclusion follows:

(A) Modern man is unhappy, more unhappy than he has ever been before. We know this from statistics on crime, divorce, alcoholism, juvenile delinquency, the

A review of *Modern Woman, The Lost Sex*, by Ferdinand Lundberg and Marynia F. Farnham.

falling birth rate. Other signs of his unhappiness are Communism, socialism, fascism, anarchism, feminism, war, and modern art.

(B) Unhappiness equals neurosis. The argument that the unhappiness apparent in such mass movements as socialism and Communism has an objective base in intolerable social conditions is readily disposed of. Material conditions have improved.

(C) Modern neurosis began with the discoveries of Copernicus. Science made man feel small by showing him that the earth was not the center of the universe. He retaliated with the assertion of his penis through the conquest of nature, the invention of machines, the industrial revolution.

(D) In the course of these compensatory activities, he unwittingly destroyed the home, replacing it with the factory as the center of his life.

(E) The devaluation of the home made woman lose her function and her sense of self-importance.

(F) Woman, to recover her prestige, began to compete with man in his own domain, to work outside the home, vote, get educated, fornicate, and neglect her children. She did all this because she grudged her husband his penis, her own vagina, with the collapse of the home, having lost its *cachet*.

(G) But woman's biological nature demands reproduction and nurture of her. It punished her for not having children, for undervaluing the home and the feminine activities (nursing, dishwashing, sewing, furniture-polishing, cooking, tutoring), by refusing her the orgasm.

(H) Statistics show that the educated (ego-striving, competitive) woman has fewer children than the uneducated woman, besides being more frigid.

(I) Woman can recapture the orgasm by accepting her biological destiny. She must have at least three children and renounce her ego-striving activities in higher education and career-seeking, except in very special instances, such as that of the female doctor. She must also renounce sexual freedom—for her always self-defeating; she should preferably be a virgin when she marries.

(J) If she fails to exemplify this rule, she will be neurotic and almost invariably frigid. Her one or two children will be socially undesirable problem-cases, phallo-narcissists like Byron, compulsive bachelor system-builders like Leibnitz or Newton, or passive-feminine males with gentle, affectionate dispositions.

(K) Naturally, however, childbearing cannot be recommended for all, but only for the "fit." About two-thirds of American women are unfit. The "fit" demonstrate their fitness by producing three children. That is, childbearing is recommended for women who bear children. For the protection of these children, spinsters should be barred from our schools, teaching posts being reserved for married women with at least one child. Bachelors should be punitively taxed.

(L) Psychotherapy is recommended for the unfit. It is expensive.

Before entering into a discussion of its contents, it must be acknowledged that this book has the crude beauties of a cartoon. The mechanical view of psychology has never been so broadly rendered. Other pictures of women vanish before a vision of The Lost Sex as a broken-down sedan with Mr. Lundberg and Dr. Farnham in mechanics' overalls peering under the hood. The frigid wife in the other twin bed will never look the same again to the husband with the psychiatric know-how. Private parts become "parts" to be sent to the psychoanalytic repair shop for reconditioning. The terminology of love and of medicine is replaced by the jargon of the factory and the garage: there is no more talk of *passion* or of *healing*, but only of *functioning* and *adjustment*. Mass production methods (statistics) yield an average woman who is tested by a bureau of standards that expects uniform "performance" —the regular production of orgasm and the regular production of children. Erraticism or failure condemns her to the junkyard of society, like an airplane grounded by the Federal Aviation Authority. The American scene takes on a new, technological desolation. This junkyard is the national eyesore, a vast dump disfiguring the suburbs of the well-regulated community, presided over by the truly feminine mother and the fully genitalized male.

To the idealized machine that is the "feminine" American woman, the husband plays a subordinate but respected part. He is converted into its servant or its tender, and to qualify him for this position, his whole life must be a character reference open to the investigation of experts. The "fully masculine male" must marry, make money, work regularly and prolifically, sustain an erection for the "normal" length of time, somewhere under half an hour. He must enjoy good health, show no feminine traits of character and have "a masterful ego-structure"; at the same time, he must not quarrel with society—radical affiliations, here as in industry, will get him dismissed as a troublemaker. Intellectual and esthetic accomplishments are not denied him, provided he is a family man, steady, with good habits, sleep-in. The author's own description of the candidate for distinction follows:

"The libidinal life of authentic genius, working with a strong, completely integrated and masterful ego-structure, is fully realized in every way. . . . The more prolific the work output of a given man, the more uniform it is in excellence and originality, the more ease there is in producing it and the higher it stands in the estimation of top workers in the field, the more likely it is to be the work of a physically healthy man. Such a man is more likely than not to be leading a sober life, married and with several children. His material establishment is apt to be better than moderately satisfactory. He never has lived in a garret. He has never had serious money difficulties, but has always been able to meet the world successfully on its own terms."

The only successful entrants mentioned by the authors are J. S. Bach and two mathematicians. Failures to qualify include Bacon, Spinoza, Schopenhauer, Rousseau, Nietzsche, Hume, Hegel, Descartes, Marx, Diderot, Napoleon, Hitler, Shelley, Keats, Coleridge, and Pascal, "much of whose work must be considered socially demoralizing." This list might be fortified by the names of Plato, Beethoven, Da Vinci, Dostoevsky, Dante, Kant, and of virtually any other great men that occur to the reader's mind. Its comparative length suggests that the problem is really one for the medieval schoolmen: that is, if by the abortion of a single Spinoza, Bacon, Descartes, et cetera, every housewife in Iowa could have an orgasm, should it be done? Fortunately, the question is indeed a scholastic one. In the practical sphere, the authors have as yet no means of enforcing the new puritanism, the puritanism of the orgasm; bachelors may, in the authors' phrase, be "suspicious" characters, and the authors may call for state-subsidized psychotherapy, but, legislators being backward, the new psychoanalytic police force has yet to be put in uniform. In the intellectual sphere, the Lundberg-Farnham argument remains purely contentious. No jot of evidence is brought forward to support the crucial proposition, that the large family and the orgasm are interdependent. College women as a group may have fewer children and be more frigid than the population as a whole, but is the college woman with three children less frigid than her classmate with none? Certainly, in the middle class, children are often the wife's excuse for terminating *amour* with her husband: don't, dear, you'll wake the baby. And the unsexed career woman may be frigid with men and amorous with women—is the Lesbian orgasm not certified by these authorities? Frigidity is a more peculiar and puzzling phenomenon than these authors admit. According to another study made by Dr. Kinsey, which has been cited to me in conversation, the female animals do not have orgasm; it is the exclusive property of the human female, who is presumed to have learned it from men. If this is so, then the biological argument is absurd, and frigidity becomes, not a hidden scandal to be exploited by sensational journalists, but a condition into which the human female rather easily, perhaps, relapses. If psychoanalysis has a cure for it, as these authors intimate, this must be the best-kept medical secret of modern times; Mr. Lundberg and Dr. Farnham, at least, are discreet enough not to introduce any evidence into the sanctuary of the assertion.

Here, as in other connections, the phrase, "clinical experience shows," relieves the authors of the necessity of proof. This phrase serves the same purpose as the photograph of the bearded doctor in the white gown extensively used in advertisements of beauty creams, reducing nostrums, and toothpaste before the passage of the Food and Drug Act. "Clinical experience," moreover, has an infinite elasticity. It shows, for example, that every child masturbates; for the patient who tells a different story, amnesia is "understood" and his failure to remember masturbating constitutes proof that he did. In the same way, clinical experience can show that a man who has intercourse several times a day is "orgastically" impotent.

For the disingenuousness of this kind of reasoning that uses its own hypothesis as proof, that appeals always to the authority of "facts" and allows itself at the same time an anarchy of interpretation, *Modern Woman, The Lost Sex* offers an unforgettable illustration. This disingenuousness, mastering contradictions, has become indifferent to them—these authors will say *anything*. Their hardened character is well exemplified by a comparison between the book jacket and pages 220 and 221 of the text. Inside, the authors are exposing the "suggestive" innuendo of contemporary advertising and pointing particularly to the use made of "illustrations of ecstatic young models half-swooning in the moonlight." Outside, on the dust-cover, is a drawing of a young model naked in the moonlight. She does not appear to be swooning but blushing. She is hiding her eyes.

April, 1947

An Academy of Risk

"This man is dangerous"—the old post-office ads alerting the community to a malefactor at large, armed and with a record, are joyously brought to mind by the bold figure of Harold Rosenberg in his book of collected essays, *The Tradition of the New*. The man who invented the term action painting is an actionist critic. All his life, as these essays show, he has been interested only in action, in the "act," a favorite word with him, succinct as a pistol-shot. Before action painting, there was the action poem (the poem as destructive agent—Baudelaire, Rimbaud, Rilke, Valéry), and political action (Marxism). To Mr. Rosenberg, action and the imitation of an action—drama—are essentially the same. He is exhilarated by the hero in history, which means that he sees history as a stage of sublime or ridiculous gestures; the hero's historical "task," what used to be called the deed, is finding the appropriate gesture. This requires a willed transformation of the merely given self, as in the evolution of the dramatic character of the Bolshevik, a secular convert; in some instances, the "transformation" may be only a disguise for a bald spot, like a toupée, which turns the historical drama into comedy. In either case, Mr. Rosenberg, who has commandeered a loge seat for the performance by

A review of *The Tradition of the New*, by Harold Rosenberg.

the authority of his intellect, genially applauds. He knows
that the problem of action is serious, dead serious for
our pistol-point time, and yet his very fascination with
the problem makes him also a critical spectator, indeed
an ideal connoisseur of the spectacle. His geniality, which
has something of the pirate in it, is a product of detachment, a quality which, contrary to common belief, is often
found in the true actionist in his moments of leisure—the
balletomane commissar, the bandit-chief in the forest
watching a Cossack sword-dance. The performer of deeds
can be objective, just because he appreciates acting. Hamlet, with the Players, got the pun too, which runs like a
mystification through language.

The great joy of this book is its zestful freedom, again
the result of objectivity. The essays, written over the
past twenty years, have been assembled in four sections,
on painting, poetry, politics, and intellectual history, and
are interrelated in a way that at first appears casual, until
the light dawns and the reader becomes aware that he is
following the greatest show on earth—the international
human comedy of modern times, a mixture of genres,
from tragedy to vaudeville, whose only heroes, finally,
are artists. Thanks to his detachment, Mr. Rosenberg
views the twentieth century as all of a piece: a century
of the new, of invention, transformation, remaking, fresh
gestures. In other words, Mr. Rosenberg's idea is that if
you don't remake yourself in this century, somebody else
will remake you—in a gas chamber. If modern history is
a panoramic stage, it is also a scientific laboratory for
the production of new human beings, new identities. The
action painter who "gesticulates" on canvas so that he
may see himself, as it were, in silhouette and discover
who he is, is experimenting on himself just as Rimbaud
did, and as the Communists did to manufacture, out of
the "iron" process of logic, the figure of the Bolshevik,
and the Nazis in their concentration-camp workshops, to
make a new "scientific" humanity—as well, incidentally,
as a new kind of lampshade. The purge indeed (Mr.
Rosenberg does not happen to mention this, but he would

surely agree) is the first obligatory step, whether it is
the infantile castor-oil purge of Mussolini, the mass
purges of the Soviet Union, the brainwashing of the Ko-
rean prisoners-of-war, the pseudo-purge of religious conversion, the prefrontal lobotomy, or the self-purgation of
the artist. Mr. Rosenberg is not afraid of this amalgam,
as it would have been called in the thirties. When Anthony
West declared in *The New Yorker* that the poems of
Baudelaire led straight to the death-camps, he was asserting in a hysterical way a Philistine and semi-totalitarian
doctrine of "responsibility"; Mr. Rosenberg sees a connection between all these modern events that is neither
causal nor criminal. His detachment permits him to ob-
serve a likeness-in-difference without feeling obliged to
confess up and withdraw his support from Rimbaud,
Baudelaire, or De Kooning.

Similarly, Mr. Rosenberg's eagle's-eye view of the twentieth century has made him the first to discern tendencies
and correspondences that became only slowly visible, if
visible at all, to other critics. In an essay on the Fall of
Paris, written in 1940, he rapidly sketches out the whole
idea of Malraux's *Musée Imaginaire* (1949); it might be
objected that Mr. Rosenberg did not "do" anything with
his idea while Malraux made a book out of it, but a better
way of putting it is that Malraux "got" a book out of it,
i.e., labored it to yield him a return. Mr. Rosenberg was
also the first to see through the guilty-liberal racket and
the mass-culture racket, in a number of essays now
grouped under the general heading, "The Herd of Independent Minds." This new body of parasitic literature—
the *True Story* confessions of ex-Communists and ex-
liberals and the mass-culture symposia—produced for
kicks for a mass audience, is itself of course a sociological
phenomenon, reflecting the vast growth of a class of professional intellectuals who are the tour-directors of modern society on a cruise looking for itself. The architects,
designers, psychiatrists, museum men, questionnaire sociologists, "depth" sociologists, students of voting habits and
population patterns, are all engaged in providing iden-

tities ("Tell me how you voted and I'll tell you who you are" or vice versa), showing their publics how they can yet be somebody through art-appreciation, music-appreciation, good-design-appreciation, self-appreciation, i.e., knowing Values. As Mr. Rosenberg says, "Today everybody is already a member of some intellectually worked-over group, that is, an audience."

Mr. Rosenberg himself is a permanent revolutionist in politics and the arts. Still, sitting in his loge seat in the intervals of partisanship, he enjoys the farce by which the New is converted into the Old, by being turned into a profit-commodity, as modern painting has been by fashion designers, educators, and wallpaper firms; this in fact is the Handwriting on the Wall. Art movements "sold" to the consumer are consumed in both senses. The position of the revolutionary critic is itself comically subject to erosion under these circumstances—a point Mr. Rosenberg has noted.

His sense of proportion and balance prevents him, almost everywhere ("Politics as Dancing" is the exception), from being mastered by one of his ideas so that he would fail to see its implications. This knowing what you are letting yourself in for constitutes audacity. Take action painting; while arguing strenuously for it, Mr. Rosenberg perceives where the hitch is. Action painting cannot lay claim to being judged aesthetically; by being an act, an experiment, it deliberately renounces the aesthetic as its category, for it cannot be recognized by the pleasure-faculty as objects of beauty are. If, indeed, by some accident—the passage of time or fading—such a painting became beautiful, it would cease to be an act, since the element of risk and hazard would depart from it, and it would come, as it were, to rest. In the same way, an act in history by becoming strikingly beautiful or noble slides out of the historical arena into a constructed frame—such actions, incidentally, are usually acts of sacrifice or heroic immolation. They become, precisely, a picture: a tableau or a statue. But if an action painting cannot be judged aesthetically, how can it be judged? Not at all, cheerfully

admits Mr. Rosenberg, though he qualifies this somewhat by saying that a genuine action painting can be told
from a fake by the amount of struggle in it. This criterion,
though, is highly arbitrary—how is the struggle to be
measured and who is to be the judge? Mr. Rosenberg,
then, is taking a risk, with his eyes open, of polemicizing
for a kind of art of which no one can say whether it is
beautiful or ugly or in between, but only that it is something, that it exists and represents a decision. This de-
cisive coming into existence, in fact, is action painting's
best plea for itself—a plea entered in history's court,
which is where Mr. Rosenberg always argues. And it is
true that the most convincing argument that can be made,
really, for action painting (Mr. Rosenberg does not make
it) is that Mr. Rosenberg himself, in his earlier essays
on poetry, described exactly those qualities that action
painting would later have. This suggests either that Mr.
Rosenberg like a god invented action painting out of
his own brain (and the movement certainly seems to have
clarified from the date of his naming it) or that its appearance was inevitable in the history of art; that is, Mr.
Rosenberg's prediction or hypothesis validates the painting, and the painting validates Mr. Rosenberg's hypothesis.
This is perhaps untenable logically, but in practice such a
coincidence really does hint that there is something to
action painting.

In Mr. Rosenberg's opinion, this painting has assumed
the binding authority of a historical necessity. We are
forced to accept it as we accept other historical changes
and advances. If we don't, we admit ourselves to the
Academy, which (excuse me, Mr. Rosenberg) seems to
me another version of the ash-can of history; if we don't
accept it, in short, we are dead. Mr. Rosenberg is at once
allured and repelled by the ever-present dead; the problem of burial is central to his book. Some of its finest
passages touch on this theme; for example this, about
Melville: ". . . while from the silent recesses of the office
files, he drew forth the white-collared tomb deity,
Bartleby." The spectral death-in-life of other contemporary

critics, moreover, is made clammily apparent by contrast with Mr. Rosenberg's own vitality. His phrasing is a gleeful boyish exploit: "it would be just as well to bump the old mob off the raft"; ". . . to the tattoo artist on Melville's Pacific Island who covered the village headman with an overall design previously tried out on some bottom dog used as a sketch pad, the problem [of the audience] did not present itself." He is picturesque without forcing, like some veteran trapper or scout chatting on in the American lingo. The range of the voice is remarkable, and so is the control of volume. The accusation sometimes made against him, that he is abstract, is absolutely untrue of his writing, which moves from graphic image to graphic image (sometimes as in a really great comic strip) and is sensitive as a hearing-aid to sound. This plain talk nearly persuades you that he is right, not only in general, but in every particular of his reasoning, for what he presents is the picture of a man in a state of buoyant health. To resist his theories at any point it is necessary to draw back from this blast of vitality and ask, for instance, whether the theory of action painting is not just a new costuming of the old Marxist myth, in which the proletariat, having so long been acted on by history, decides to act into history and abolish it. By the violence of his "attack" on the canvas, the action painter abolishes art. But is it really possible to abolish art? Will not the aesthetic as a category of human experience perversely assert itself, as history did in the Soviet Union by refusing to come to an end? This in fact is happening to the school of action painters and was bound to happen regardless of the activities of museum people and popularizers. Once you hang an act on your living-room wall, a weird contradiction develops, which is inherent in the definition (or myth) of action painting itself; an "event" or gesture becomes, at worst, just as much an art-object as the piece of driftwood on the coffee table or the seashell on the Victorian whatnot. At best, it becomes art. The truth is, you cannot hang an event on the wall, only a picture, which may be found to be beautiful or ugly, de-

pending, alas, on your taste. This applies to a Cimabue
"Crucifixion" just as much as to a Pollock or an African
mask. You can decide of a new painting or a painting
new to you that it is "interesting," but this only means
that you are postponing, for the moment, the harder decision as to whether it is good or bad; a painting cannot
stay "interesting," or if you keep on calling it that you
have made "interesting" into an aesthetic judgment—a
judgment, by the way, which leads, by the broad path, to
the populous cemetery of the Academy, where all but
the immortal are buried by Father Time.

Summer, 1959

The Fact in Fiction

I am scheduled, I find, to talk to you about "Problems of Writing a Novel." Where this title originated no one seems to know—doubtless in the same bureau that supplies titles for school children's compositions: "How I Spent My Summer Vacation" or "Adventures of a Penny" or simply "Why?" The problems of writing a novel, to those who do not write, can be reduced to the following questions: "Do you write in longhand or on the typewriter?" "Do you use an outline or do you invent as you go along?" "Do you draw your characters from real life or do you make them up or are they composites?" "Do you start with an idea, a situation, or a character?" "How many hours a day do you spend at your desk?" "Do you write on Sundays?" "Do you revise as you go along or finish a whole draft first?" And, finally, "Do you use a literary agent or do you market your stuff yourself?" Here curiosity fades; the manufacture and marketing of the product complete the story of a process, which is not essentially different from the "story" of flour as demonstrated to a class of boys and girls on an educational trip through a flour mill (from the grain of wheat to the sack on the grocer's shelf) or the "story" of a bottle of claret or of a brass safety pin. This is the craft of fiction, insofar as it

This is a paraphrase of a talk or talks given to Polish, Yugoslav, and British audiences in the winter of 1960.

interests the outsider, who may line up, after a lecture like this, to get the author's autograph, in lieu of a free sample—a miniature bottle of wine or a card of "baby" safety pins.

Now I am not going to talk about the problems of the novel in this sense at all but rather to confront the fact that the writing of a novel has become problematic today. Is it still possible to write novels—in longhand or on the typewriter, standing or sitting, on Sundays or weekdays, with or without an outline? The answer, it seems to me, is certainly not yes and perhaps, tentatively, no. I mean real novels—not fairy tales or fables or romances or *contes philosophiques,* and I mean novels of a high order, like *War and Peace* or *Middlemarch* or *Ulysses* or the novels of Dickens, Dostoevsky, or Proust. The manufacture of second-rate novels, or, rather, of facsimiles of the novel, is in no state of crisis; nor is there a difficulty in marketing them, with or without an agent. But almost no writer in the West of any consequence, let us say since the death of Thomas Mann, has been able to write a true novel; the exception is Faulkner, who is now an old man. What was the last novel, not counting Faulkner, that was written in our day? *Ulysses? Man's Fate?* Camus' *The Stranger?* Someone might say *Lolita,* and perhaps it is a novel, a freak, though, a sport or wild mutation, which everyone approaches with suspicion, as if it were a dangerous conundrum, a Sphinx's riddle.

What do I mean by a "novel"? A prose book of a certain thickness that tells a story of real life. No one could disagree with that, and yet many will disagree with much that I am going to say before I am through, so I shall try to be more specific. The words "prose" and "real" are crucial to my conception of the novel. The distinctive mark of the novel is its concern with the actual world, the world of fact, of the verifiable, of figures, even, and statistics. If I point to Jane Austen, Dickens, Balzac, George Eliot, Tolstoy, Dostoevsky, the Melville of *Moby Dick,* Proust, the Joyce of *Ulysses,* Dreiser, Faulkner, it will be admitted that they are all novelists and that, different as they are from a formal point of view, they have one thing in common: a deep love of fact, of the empiric element in experience. I am not interested in making a formal definition of the novel (it is really a very loose affair, a grabbag or portmanteau, as someone has said) but in finding its *quidditas* or whatness, the essence or binder that distinguishes it from other species of prose fiction: the tale, the fable, the romance. The staple ingredient present in all novels in various mixtures and proportions but always in fairly heavy dosage is fact.

If a criterion is wanted for telling a novel from a fable or a tale or a romance (or a drama), a simple rule-of-thumb would be the absence of the supernatural. In fables and fairy tales, as everyone knows, birds and beasts talk. In novels, they don't; if you find birds and beasts talking in a book you are reading you can be sure it is not a novel. That takes care, for example, of *Animal Farm*. Men in novels may behave like beasts, but beasts in novels may not behave like men. That takes care of *Gulliver's Travels,* in case anyone were to mistake it for a novel. The characters in a novel must obey the laws of nature. They cannot blow up or fly or rise from the dead, as they can in plays, and if they talk to the devil, like Ivan Karamazov, the devil, though he speaks French, is not real like Faust's Mephistopheles, but a product of Ivan's derangement or fissionization. The devil is a part of Ivan. In the same way, in Mann's *Dr. Faustus,* the devil is no longer a member of the cast of characters but resident, you might say, in the fatal spirochete or syphilis germ. This is not a difference in period; Goethe did not believe in real devils either, but he could put one on the stage, because the stage accepts devils and even has a trapdoor ready for them to disappear through, with a flash of brimstone, just as it used to have a machine, up in the flies, for the gods to descend from. There are no gods in the novel and no machinery for them; to speak, even metaphorically, of a *deus ex machina* in a novel— that is, of the entrance of a providential figure from above —is to imply a shortcoming; Dickens is always criticized on this score. But a tale almost requires the appearance of a *deus ex machina* or magic helper. The devil can appear in person in a tale of Hawthorne's like "Young Goodman Brown," but not in Hawthorne's novel, *The Scarlet Letter,* though he may be there in spirit.

The novel does not permit occurrences outside the order of nature—miracles. Mr. Krook's going up in spontaneous combustion in his junkshop is a queer Punch-and-Judy note in *Bleak House.* Actually, Dickens thought science had found out that people could explode of their own force, but now it seems that they can't, that Mr. Krook couldn't; it would be all right in a fantasy or a pantomime but not in a novel. You remember how in *The Brothers Karamazov* when Father Zossima dies, his faction (most of the sympathetic characters in the book) expects a miracle: that his body will stay sweet and fresh because he died "in the odor of sanctity." But instead he begins to stink. The stink of Father Zossima is the natural, generic smell of the novel.

By the same law, a novel cannot be laid in the future, since the future, until it happens, is outside the order of nature; no prophecy or cautionary tale like *1984* is a novel. It is the same with public events in the past that never happened, for example the mutiny at the end of World War I led by a Christlike corporal in Faulkner's *A Fable;* the title is Faulkner's warning to his readers that this volume, unlike his "regular" books, is not to be considered a novel but something quite different. Because the past appears, through recession, to be outside the order of nature (think how improbable and ghostly old photographs look), most historical novels, so-called, are romances, not novels: George Eliot's *Romola* in contrast to *Middlemarch.* This rule is broken by Tolstoy's *War and Peace,* a novel if there ever was one, and the reason for this is that history, as it were, has been purged by Tolstoy's harsh and critical realism of all "historical" elements—the flummery of costume, make-up, and accessories and the myths and lies of historians. The time, moreover (his grandfather's day) was not very remote from

Tolstoy's own. When he experimented with writing a novel about the days of Ivan the Terrible, he found he could not do it. A borderline case is Stendhal's *The Charterhouse of Parma,* where actual history (Napoleon's entry into Milan; the Battle of Waterloo, so much admired by Tolstoy) is succeeded by mock-history—the spurious history of Parma, complete with numbered despots, prisons, and paid assassins, a travesty invented by Stendhal to correspond with the (literally) travestied Fabrizio in his violet stockings and with the mock-heroics of this section of the book. The book is a novel that turns into parody at the moment that history, in Stendhal's opinion, ceased to make sense and turned into a parody of the past. That moment was the triumph of reaction in Europe after 1815.

I ought to make it clear that these distinctions are in no way pejorative; I do not mean "Novel good, fable bad," merely "Novel novel; fable fable." *Candide* is not a novel, but to say so is not a criticism of *Candide.* Indeed, there are certain masterpieces—Rameau's *Nephew* Gogol's *Dead Souls, The Charterhouse of Parma* itself—so quicksilver in their behavior that it is impossible to catch them in a category; these are usually "destructive" books, like *Candide,* where the author's aim is, among other things, to elude the authorities' grasp. When people nowadays tell you something is "not a novel," as they are fond of saying, for instance, about *Dr. Zhivago,* it is always in a querulous tone, as though someone had tried to put something over on them, sell them the Empire State Building or Trajan's Monument or the Palace of Culture, when *they* know better; they were not born yesterday. That is not my intention; I am not speaking as an aggrieved consumer of modern literature (and I admire *Dr. Zhivago* too passionately to demand its identity papers before I will let it pass); I am only trying to see why a special kind of literature, a relatively new kind, what we call the novel, is disappearing from view. To do that, I must know what the novel is; it is like advertising for a missing person; first you need a description of what he looked like when last seen.

Let me begin with the birthmarks. The word novel goes back to the word "new," and in the plural it used to mean news—the news of the day or the year. Literary historians find the seed or the germ of the novel in Boccaccio's *Decameron,* a collection of tales set in a frame of actual life. This frame of actual life was the Great Plague of 1348 as it affected the city of Florence, where more than a hundred thousand people died between March and August. The figures and dates come from *The Decameron,* along with a great deal of other factual information about the Black Death: its origin in the East, some years before; its primary and secondary symptoms, differing from those in the East; the time between the appearance of the first symptoms—the tumors or buboes in the groin or armpits, some the size of a common apple, some of an egg, some larger, some smaller—and the onset of death; the means of contagion; the sanitary precautions taken; the medical theories current as to the proper diet and mode of life to stave off infection; the modes of nursing; the rites and methods of burial; and, finally, the moral behavior (very bad) of the citizens of Florence during the scourge. Boccaccio's account is supposed to be a pioneer contribution to descriptive medicine; it is also a piece of eyewitness journalism, not unlike the Younger Pliny's account of the eruption of Mount Vesuvius; the difference is that Pliny wrote his report in a letter (a classic literary form) and that Boccaccio's report is used in a new way, as a setting for a collection of fictions. The "realism," also new, of the separate tales, is grounded, so to speak, in the journalistic frame, with the dateline of a certain Tuesday morning, of the year 1348, when seven young ladies, between the ages of eighteen and twenty-eight, and three young men, the youngest twenty-five, met in the Church of Santa Maria Novella.

If Boccaccio is the ancestor, the "father of the modern novel" is supposed to be Defoe, a Grub Street journalist, and the author of *Robinson Crusoe, Moll Flanders,* and many other works, including *The Journal of the Plague Year* (not Boccaccio's; another one—1664–1665). *Rob-*

inson Crusoe was based on "a real life story," of a round-the-world voyage, which he heard described by the returned traveler and which he pieced out with another, a written account. Not only was the "father of the modern novel" a journalist, but he did not distinguish, at least to his readers, between journalism and fiction. All his stories pretend to be factual reports, documents, and one perhaps is—the life of a famous criminal "as told to Daniel Defoe," i.e., ghost-written. This pretense, which might be called the reverse of plagiarism, the disclaiming, that is, of authorship rather than the claiming of it, was not a special pathological kink of Defoe's. The novel in its early stages almost always purports to be true. Where a fairy tale begins, "Once upon a time, in a certain kingdom," a tale of Boccaccio (chosen at random) begins: "You must know that after the death of Emperor Frederick II, the crown of Sicily passed to Manfred, whose favor was enjoyed to the highest degree by a gentleman of Naples, Arrighetto Capece by name, who had to wife Madonna Beritola Caracciola, a fair and gracious lady, likewise a Neapolitan. Now when Manfred was conquered and slain by King Charles I at Benevento . . . Arrighetto, etc., etc. . . ." The effect of this naming and placing makes of every story of Boccaccio's a sort of deposition, and this is even truer when the sphere is less exalted and the place is a neighboring village and the hero a well-known lecherous priest.

Many of the great novelists were newspaper reporters or journalists. Dickens had been a parliamentary reporter as a young man; in middle age, he became a magazine editor, and the scent of a "news story" is keen in all his novels. Dostoevsky, with his brother, edited two different magazines, one of which was called *Time* (*Vremya*); he supplied them with fiction and feature stories, and his specialty, you might say, was police reporting—he visited suspects (usually female) in prison, interviewed them, and wrote up his impressions; he also reported trials. Victor Hugo too was a confirmed prison-visitor; his "impressions" of prisons and of current political events—demonstrations, tumults, street-fighting—are collected in *Choses Vues*. Tolstoy first became widely known through his reports from Sebastopol, where he was serving as a young officer in the Crimean War; he was telling the news, the true, uncensored story of the Siege of Sebastopol, to the civilians back home, and throughout Tolstoy's work, most noticeably in *War and Peace* but in fact everywhere, there is heard the scathing directness of the young officer's tone, calling attention to the real facts behind the official dispatches—the real facts of war, sex, family life, glory, love, death. As he wrote in his second sketch from Sebastopol (which was immediately suppressed by the Czar), "The hero of my story . . . is—the Truth." Coming to the twentieth century, you meet the American novelist as newspaperman: Dreiser, Sinclair Lewis, Hemingway, O'Hara, Faulkner himself. The American novelist as newspaperman, in the twenties, became a stock figure in the American myth, so much so that the terms could be inverted and every obscure newspaperman, according to popular belief, had in his desk drawer, besides a pint of whiskey, the great American novel he was writing in his spare time.

There is another kind of "fact" literature closely related to the novel, and that is the travel book, which tells the news of the exotic. Melville's first book, *Typee*, was a book of travel, and you find something of the travelogue in Conrad, Kipling, and a good deal of D. H. Lawrence: *Aaron's Rod, The Plumed Serpent, Kangaroo,* "The Woman Who Rode Away." There is very little difference, really, between *Kangaroo,* a novel about Australia, and *Sea and Sardinia,* a travel book about Lawrence himself and Frieda in Sardinia. Hemingway remains half a war correspondent and half an explorer; *The Green Hills of Africa* is his "straight" travel book. The type seems to go back to *Robinson Crusoe;* most of Conrad's heroes, one could say, are stranded Robinson Crusoes, demoralized by consciousness. In a more conventional way, Dickens, Stendhal, Henry James all published journals of travel—"impressions." Mark Twain, Henry Miller, George Orwell (*Down and Out in Paris and London, Shooting an*

Elephant)—the list is even more arresting if you consider the theatre and try to imagine Ibsen, Shaw, or O'Neill as the authors of travel books. Yet Ibsen spent years abroad, in Italy and Germany, and O'Neill, like Melville and Conrad, went to sea as a young man.

The passion for fact in a raw state is a peculiarity of the novelist. Most of the great novels contain blocks and lumps of fact—refractory lumps in the porridge of the story. Students often complain of this in the old novels. They skip these "boring parts" to get on with the story, and in America a branch of publishing specializes in short-ened versions of novels—"cut for greater reading speed." Descriptions and facts are eliminated, and only the pure story, as it were the scenario, is left. But a novel that was only a scenario would not be a novel at all.

Everyone knows that Balzac was a lover of fact. He delighted in catalogues of objects, inventories, explanations of the way institutions and industries work, how art is collected, political office is bought, fortunes are amassed or hoarded. One of his novels, *Les Illusions Perdues*, has a chapter which simply describes the way paper is made. The chapter has nothing to do with the action of the novel (it comes in because the hero has inherited a paper factory); Balzac put it in because he happened at the time to know something about the paper business. He loved facts of every kind indiscriminately—straight facts, curious facts, quirks, oddities, aberrations of fact, figures, statistics. He collected them and stored them, like one of his own misers, intending to house them in that huge structure, *The Human Comedy,* which is at once a scale model of the real world and a museum of curios left to mankind as though by a crazy hermit who could never throw anything away.

This fetishism of fact is generally treated as a sort of disease of realism of which Balzac was the prime clinical exhibit. But this is not the case. You find the splendid sickness in realists and nonrealists alike. *Moby Dick,* among other things, is a compendium of everything that was to be known about whaling. The chapters on the whale and on whiteness, which are filled with curious lore, truths that are "stranger than fiction," interrupt and "slow down" the narrative, like the excursus on paper. Yet they cannot be taken away (as the excursus on paper certainly could be) without damaging the novel; *Moby Dick* without these chapters (in the stage and screen versions) is not *Moby Dick*. Or think of the long chapter on the Russian Monk in *The Brothers Karamazov*. Father Zossima is about to enter the scene, and, before introducing him, Dostoevsky simply stops and writes a history of the role of the elder in Russian monasticism. In the same way, in *War and Peace,* when Pierre gets interested in Freemasonry, Tolstoy stops and writes an account of the Masonic movement, for which he had been boning up in the library. Everyone who has read *War and Peace* remembers the Battle of Borodino, the capture and firing of Moscow, the analysis of the character of Napoleon, the analysis of the causes of war, and the great chapter on Freedom and Necessity, all of which are nonfiction and which constitute the very terrain of the novel; indeed, it could be said that the real plot of *War and Peace* is the struggle of the characters not to be immersed, engulfed, swallowed up by the landscape of fact and "history" in which they, like all human beings, have been placed: freedom (the subjective) is in the fiction, and necessity is in the fact. I have already mentioned the first chapter of *The Charterhouse of Parma* describing Napoleon's entry into Milan. In *The Magic Mountain,* there are the famous passages on tuberculosis, recalling Boccaccio's description of the plague, and the famous chapter on time, a philosophical excursus like the chapter on whiteness in *Moby Dick* and the chapter on Freedom and Necessity in Tolstoy. Closer to Balzac is Dreiser's picture of the hotel business in *An American Tragedy;* when Clyde becomes a bellhop, Dreiser (though this is not "important" to the story) stops and shows the reader how a hotel, behind the scenes, works.

In newspaper jargon, you might call all this the boiler plate of the novel—durable informative matter set up in stereotype and sold to country newspapers as filler to eke out a scarcity of local news, i.e., of "plot." And the novel, like newspaper boiler plate, contained not only a miscellany of odd facts but household hints and how-to-do-it instructions (you can learn how to make strawberry jam from *Anna Karenina* and how to reap a field and hunt ducks).

The novel, to repeat, has or had many of the functions of a newspaper. Dickens' novels can be imagined in terms of headlines: "Antique Dealer Dies by Spontaneous Combustion in Shop," "Financial Wizard Falls, Panic Among Speculators," "Blackleg Miner Found Dead in Quarry." Henry James, who did his best to exclude every bit of boiler plate from his books and who may have killed the novel, perhaps with kindness (consider the unmentionable small article manufactured by the Newsomes in *The Ambassadors;* what was it? Garters? Safety pins?), even James has the smell of newsprint about him, the smell of the Sunday supplement. His international plots recall the magazine section of the old Hearst newspaper chain, in which every Sunday, after church, Americans used to read about some international marriage between an American heiress and a titled fortune-hunter: Anna Gould and Count Boni de Castellane.

Novels, including James's, carried the news—of crime, high society, politics, industry, finance, and low life. In Dickens you find a journalistic coverage of the news on all fronts and a survey of all the professions from pick-pocket to banker, from lawyer to grave-robber. His books tell the whole story of Victorian society, from the front page to the financial section. This ideal of coverage requires him, in fairness, to print, as it were, corrections; a bad Jew is followed by a good Jew, a bad lawyer by a good one, a bad school by a good one, and so on. Or, to put it another way, it is as though he were launching a great roomy Noah's Ark with two of each species of creation aboard. In a single book, *Middlemarch,* George Eliot "covers" English life and institutions, as found at their median point—a middling provincial town. The notion of coverage by professions was taken up, somewhat mechanically, by the American novelists Dreiser and Sinclair Lewis. You can hear it in Dreiser's titles: *The Titan, The Financier, The Genius, Twelve Men*. Lewis ticked off the housewife (*Main Street*), the realtor (*Babbitt*), the scientist (*Arrowsmith*), the preacher (*Elmer Gantry*), the social worker (*Ann Vickers*), the retired businessman (*Dodsworth*). A similar census, though of more mobile social types, is seen in Dos Passos. It is Faulkner, however, the most "mythic" of recent American novelists, who has documented a society more completely than any of the realists. Like Dickens, he has set himself the task of a Second Creation. Yoknapatawpha County, capital, Jefferson), Mississippi, is presided over by its courthouse (*Requiem for a Nun*), where its history and vital statistics are on file; we know its population of lawyers, storekeepers, businessmen, farmers, black and white, and their forebears and how they made or lost their money; we know its idiots and criminals and maniacs, its geology and geography, flora and fauna (the bear of that story and the cow of *The Hamlet*); some editions of Faulkner include a map of Yoknapatawpha County, and a letter addressed to Faulkner at Jefferson, Mississippi, would almost certainly reach him, although there is no such place.

The more poetic a novel, the more it has the air of being a factual document. I exaggerate when I say this, but if you think of Faulkner, of *Moby Dick,* of *Madame Bovary* or Proust, you will see there is something in it. Joyce's *Ulysses* is a case in point. There is no doubt that Joyce intended to reconstruct, almost scientifically, twenty-four hours of a certain day in Dublin; the book, among other things, is an exercise in mnemonics. Stephen and Mr. Bloom, in their itineraries, cover certain key points in the life of the city—the beach, the library, the graveyard, the cabman's stand, Nighttown—and a guide to Joyce's Dublin has been published, with maps and a key. Nor is it by chance that the peripatetic Mr. Bloom is an advertising *canvasser*. He travels back and forth and up and down in society like Ulysses, who explored the four corners of the known world. The epic, I might put in here, is the form of all literary forms closest to the novel; it has the "boiler plate," the lists and catalogues, the circumstantiality, the concern with numbers and dimensions. The epic geography, like that of the novel, can be *mapped,* in both the physical and the social sense.

This clear locative sense is present in all true novels. Take Jane Austen. *Emma* and *Pride and Prejudice* contain few facts of the kind I have been speaking of—nothing like the paper business or the history of the Russian monk. Yet there are facts of a different sort, documents like Mr. Collins' letters, charades, riddles, menus, dance programs (" 'Then the two third he danced with Miss King, and the two fourth with Maria Lucas, and the two fifth with Jane again, and the two sixth with Lizzy, and the *Boulanger*—' ")—feminine facts, so to speak—and a very painstaking census-taking of a genteel class within the confines of a certain income range, marked off, like a frontier. One difference between Jane Austen and Henry James is that the reader of *Pride and Prejudice* knows exactly how much money the characters have: Mr. Bingley has four or five thousand a year (with a capital of nearly one hundred thousand); Mr. Bennet has two thousand a year, ENTAILED, while Mrs. Bennet brought him a capital of four thousand from her father, an attorney at Meryton; Mr. Darcy has ten thousand a year; his sister, Georgiana, has a capital of thirty thousand. The same with distances, ages, and time. Mr. and Mrs. Bennet have been married twenty-three years; Mrs. Weston, in *Emma,* has been Emma's governess for sixteen years; Mr. Knightley is about seven or eight and thirty; Emma is nearly twenty-one; Jane and Elizabeth, when they are finally married, live thirty miles apart; Highbury is about a mile from Mr. Knightley's property. Whenever the chance arises, Jane Austen supplies a figure. Everything is lucid and perspicuous in her well-charted world, except the weather, which is often unsettled, and this fact too is always noted ("The shower was heavy but short, and it had not been over five minutes when . . ."). The names of persons who are never seen in the story, like that of "Miss King" just now, are dropped as if artlessly to attest the veracity of the narrative—inviting the reader to clothe these names himself with the common identities of real life.

This air of veracity is very important to the novel. We do really (I think) expect a novel to be true, not only true to itself, like a poem, or a statue, but true to actual life, which is right around the corner, like the figure of "Miss King." We not only make believe we believe a novel, but we do substantially believe it, as being continuous with real life, made of the same stuff, and the presence of fact in fiction, of dates and times and distances, is a kind of reassurance—a guarantee of credibility. If we read a novel, say, about conditions in postwar Germany, we expect it to be an accurate report of conditions in postwar Germany; if we find out that it is not, the novel is discredited. This is not the case with a play or a poem. Dante can be wrong in *The Divine Comedy;* it does not matter, with Shakespeare, that Bohemia has no seacoast, but if Tolstoy was all wrong about the Battle of Borodino or the character of Napoleon, *War and Peace* would suffer.

The presence of a narrator, writing in the first person, is another guarantee of veracity. The narrator is, precisely, an eyewitness, testifying to the reader that these things really happened, even though the reader knows of course that they did not. This is the function of the man called Marlow in Conrad's books; he is there to promise the reader that these faraway stories are true, and, as if Marlow himself were not enough, the author appears as a kind of character witness for Marlow, testifying to having met him in reliable company, over cigars, claret, a polished mahogany table, and so on. The same function is served by the narrator in Dostoevsky's *The Possessed,* who writes in the excited manner of a small-town gossip ("Then I rushed to Varvara Petrovna's") telling you everything that went on in that extraordinary period, which everybody in town is still talking about, that began when young Stavrogin bit the governor's ear. He tells what he saw himself and what he had on hearsay and pretends to sift the collective evidence as to what exactly happened and in what order. Faulkner's favorite narrator is Gavin Stevens, the lawyer, chosen obviously because the town lawyer, accustomed to weighing evidence, would be the most reliable witness—one of the first sources a newspaper reporter sent to do a story on Yoknapatawpha County would be likely to consult.

There is the shadow of an "I" in *The Brothers Karamazov,* but *The Possessed* is the only important novel of Dostoevsky's that is told straight through in the first person, i.e., by a local busybody who seems to have seized the pen. *The Possessed* (in Russian *The Devils*) is the most demonic of all Dostoevsky's novels—the most "unnatural," unfilial, "Gothic." It would seem that the device of the narrator, the eyewitness "I," like Esther Summerson in *Bleak House* (not the autobiographical "I" of *David Copperfield* or of Proust's Marcel, who is something more than a witness), is more often used in novels whose material is exotic or improbable than in the plain novel of ordinary life, like *Middlemarch* or *Emma* or any of Trollope. These novels of ordinary life put no strain on the reader's credulity; he believes without the testimony of witnesses. The first-person narrator is found in Conrad, in Melville, and in *Wuthering Heights, Bleak House, Jane Eyre,* all of which center around drafty, spooky old houses and are related to the ghost story. In the same way James, who rarely used the first-person narrator, does so with the governess in his ghost story, *The Turn of the Screw.* In other words, on the periphery of the novel, on the borderline of the tale or the adventure story you find a host of narrators. And you arrive, finally, at *Lolita* and meet Humbert Humbert, telling his own story (which you might not have believed otherwise), having been first introduced by another narrator, his "editor," who authenticates his manuscript; Humbert

himself has been executed. In short, you are back with
Defoe and his "true biographies" of great criminals who
were hanged, back at the birth of the novel, before it
could stand without support.

Even when it is more serious, the novel's characteristic
tone is one of gossip and tittletattle. You can hear it in
the second sentence (originally the first sentence) of
Anna Karenina: "Everything was upset at the Oblon-
skys'." The cook, it seemed, had left; the underservants
had given notice; the mistress was shut up in her bed-
room because the master had been sleeping with the former French governess. This (I think) is a classic beginning, and yet some person who had never read a novel,
coming on those sentences, so full of blunt malice, might
conclude that Tolstoy was simply a common scandal-
monger. The same might be thought of Dostoevsky, of
Flaubert, Stendhal, and (obviously) of Proust, of the
earnest George Eliot and the lively Jane Austen and the
manly Charles Dickens. Most of these writers were people of high principle; their books, without exception, had
a moral, ethical, or educational purpose. But the voice
we overhear in their narratives, if we stop to listen for a
minute, putting aside preconceptions, is the voice of a
neighbor relating the latest gossip. "You will hardly believe what happened next," the novelists from Jane
Austen to Kafka (yes indeed) seem to be exclaiming.
"Wait and I'll tell you." The whole narrative method of
Dostoevsky could be summed up in those two sentences.
In Conrad, more ruminative, there can be heard the
creaking of chairs as the men around the table settle
down to listen to the indefatigable Marlow, who only
halts to wet his whistle: "Pass the bottle." The scandals
the novelists are primed with are the scandals of a village, a town, or a province—Highbury or Jefferson, Mississippi, or the Province of O——; the scandals of a
clique—the Faubourg St. Germain; of a city—Dublin or
Middlemarch; or of a nation—Dickens' England; or of
the ports and hiring offices—London or Nantucket, where

news of the high seas is exchanged and a black mark put against a man's name or a vessel's. Here is another criterion: if the breath of scandal has not touched it, the book is not a novel. That is the trouble with the art-novel (most of Virginia Woolf, for instance); it does not stoop to gossip.

The scandals of a village or a province, the scandals of a nation or of the high seas feed on facts and breed speculation. But it is of the essence of a scandal that it be finite, for all its repercussions and successive enlargements. Indeed, its repercussions are like the echo produced in an enclosed space, a chambered world. That is why institutions ("closed corporations") are particularly prone to scandal; they attempt to keep the news in, contain it, and in doing so they magnify it, and then, as people say, "the lid is off." It is impossible, except for theologians, to conceive of a world-wide scandal or a universe-wide scandal; the proof of this is the way people have settled down to living with nuclear fission, radiation poisoning, hydrogen bombs, satellites, and space rockets. Nobody can get them excited about or even greatly interested in what-will-happen-next to the world; the plot does not thicken. In the same way, Hiroshima, despite the well-meant efforts of journalists and editors, probably caused less stir than the appearance of comets in the past; the magnitude of the event killed even curiosity. This was true, to some extent, of Buchenwald and Auschwitz too.

Yet these "scandals," in the theological sense, of the large world and the universe have dwarfed the finite scandals of the village and the province; who cares any more what happens in Highbury or the Province of O——? If the novelist cares, he blushes for it; that is, he blushes for his parochialism. *Middlemarch* becomes *Middletown* and *Middletown in Transition,* the haunt of social scientists, whose factual findings, even in the face of Auschwitz or a space-satellite, have a certain cachet because they are supposed to be "science"; in science, all facts, no matter how trivial or banal, enjoy democratic equality. Among novelists, it is only Faulkner who does not seem to feel an itch of dissatisfaction with his sphere, and there are signs of this even in him—*A Fable,* for example.

But it is not only that the novelist of today, in "our expanding universe," is embarrassed by the insignificance (or lack of "significance") of his finite world. A greater problem is that he cannot quite believe in it. That is, the existence of Highbury or the Province of O—— is rendered improbable, unveracious, by Buchenwald and Auschwitz, the population curve of China, and the hydrogen bomb. Improbable when "you stop to think"; this is the experience of everybody and not only of the novelist; if we stop to think for one second, arrested by some newspaper story or general reflection, our daily life becomes incredible to us. I remember reading the news of Hiroshima in a little general store on Cape Cod in Massachusetts and saying to myself as I moved up to the counter, "What am I doing buying a loaf of bread?" The coexistence of the great world and us, when contemplated, appears impossible.

It works both ways. The other side of the picture is that Buchenwald and Auschwitz are and were unbelievable, and not just to the German people, whom we criticize for forgetting them; we all forget them, as we forget the hydrogen bomb, because their special quality is to stagger belief. And here is the dilemma of the novelist, which is only a kind of professional sub-case of the dilemma of everyone: if he writes about his province, he feels its inverisimilitude; if he tries, on the other hand, to write about people who make lampshades of human skin, like the infamous Ilse Koch, he feels still more the inverisimilitude of what he is asserting. His love of truth revolts. And yet this love of truth, ordinary common truth recognizable to everyone, is the ruling passion of the novel. Putting two and two together, then, it would seem that the novel, with its common sense, is of all forms the least adapted to encompass the modern world, whose leading characteristic is irreality. And that, so far as I can understand, is why the novel is dying. The souped-up novels that are being written today, with injections of myth and symbols to heighten or "deepen" the material, are simply evasions and forms of self-flattery.

I spoke just now of common sense—the prose of the novel. We are all supposed to be born with it, in some degree, but we are also supposed to add to it by experience and observation. But if the world today has become inaccessible to common sense, common sense in terms of broad experience simultaneously has become inaccessible to the writer. The novelists of the nineteenth century had, both as public persons and private figures, great social range; they "knew everybody," whether because of their fame in the great capitals of London, Paris, St. Petersburg, or in their village, province, or county, where everybody knows everybody as a matter of course. Today the writer has become specialized, like the worker on an assembly line whose task is to perform a single action several hundred times a day or the doctor whose task is to service a single organ of the human body. The writer today is turning into a *machine à ecrire,* a sort of human typewriter with a standardized mechanical output: hence the meaning of those questions ("How many hours a day?" "How long does it take you?" "Have you ever thought of using a dictaphone?"). This standardization and specialization is not only a feature of his working hours but of his social existence. The writer today— and especially the young American writer—sees only other writers; he does not know anyone else. His social circle comprises other writers and his girl friends, but his girl friends, usually, are hoping to be writers too. The writer today who has a painter for a friend is regarded as a broad-ranging adventurer, a real man of the world. If he teaches in a university, his colleagues are writers or at any rate they "publish," and his students, like his girl friends, are hoping to write themselves. This explains the phenomenon, often regarded as puzzling, of the "one-book" American writer, the writer who starts out with promise and afterward can only repeat himself or fade away. There is nothing puzzling about it; he wrote that first book before he became a writer, while he was still an ordinary person. The worst thing, I would say, that can happen to a writer today is to become a writer. And it is most fatal of all for the novelist; the poet can survive it, for he does not need social range for his verse, and poets have always clubbed together with other poets in exclusive coteries, which is perhaps why Plato wanted them banned from the Republic.

The isolation of the modern writer is a social fact, and not just the writer's own willful fault. He cannot help being "bookish," which cuts him off from society, since practically the only people left who read are writers, their wives and girl friends, teachers of literature, and students hoping to become writers. The writer has "nothing in common" with the businessman or the worker, and this is almost literally true; there is no common world left in which they share. The businessman who does not read is just as specialized as the writer who writes.

To throw off this straitjacket is the recurrent dream of the modern novelist, after the age, say, of thirty or thirty-five; before that, his dream was the opposite: to come to New York (or Paris or London) to meet other writers. Various ways out are tried: moving to the country, travel, "action" (some form of politics), the resolute cultivation of side-interests—music, art, sport, gardening; sport is very popular with American men novelists, who hold on to an interest in baseball or a tennis racket or a fishing-rod as a relic of the "complete man" or complete boy they once were. But if these steps are sufficiently radical, their effect may be the reverse of what was intended. This is what seems to have happened to Gide, D. H. Lawrence, Malraux, Camus, George Orwell. Starting as novelists, they fled, as it were, in all directions

from the tyranny of the novelist's specialization: into
politics, diary-keeping, travel and travel-writing, war, art
history, journalism, "engagement." Nor did they ever
really come back to the novel, assuming that was what
they wanted to do. Gide stopped with *The Counter-
feiters;* Lawrence with *Women in Love;* Malraux with
Man's Fate; Orwell with his first book, *Burmese Days;*
Camus with *The Stranger.* Their later books are not
novels, even if they are called so, but fables of various
kinds, tracts, and parables. But they did not settle down
to a single form or mode, and this perpetual restlessness
which they have in common seems a sign of an unre-
quited, unconsummated love for the novel, as though in
the middle of their *oeuvre* there were a void, a blank
space reserved for the novel they failed to be able to
write. We think of them as among the principal "novelists" of our time, but they were hardly novelists at all,
and in each case their work as a whole has an air of
being unfinished, dangling.

They are certainly key modern figures. Allowing for
differences in talent, their situation is everybody's; mine
too. We are all in flight from the novel and yet drawn
back to it, as to some unfinished and problematic relation-
ship. The novel seems to be dissolving into its component
parts: the essay, the travel book, reporting, on the one
hand, and the "pure" fiction of the tale, on the other. The
center will not hold. No structure (except Faulkner's) has
been strong enough to keep in suspension the diverse elements of which the novel is made. You can call this, if
you want, a failure of imagination. We know that the real
world exists, but we can no longer imagine it.

Yet despite all I have been saying, I cannot, being
human, help feeling that the novel is not finished yet. Tomorrow is another day. Someone, somewhere, even now
may be dictating into a dictaphone: "At five o'clock in
the afternoon, in the capital of the Province of Y——, a
tall man with an umbrella was knocking at the door of

the governor's residence." In short, someone may be able
to believe again in the reality, the factuality, of the world.

Summer, 1960

Characters in Fiction

In Belgrade, the other day, an interviewer asked me what book I thought best represented the modern American woman. All I could think of to answer was: *Madame Bovary*. It occurred to me afterward that I might have named *Main Street* or Henry James's *A Portrait of a Lady*. What else? I tried to remember women in American books. Hester Prynne, Daisy Miller, Scott Fitzgerald's flappers and Daisy in *The Great Gatsby,* Temple Drake in *Sanctuary,* Dos Passos' career women, Ma Joad in *The Grapes of Wrath*. But since then? It was like leafing through a photograph album and coming, midway, on a sheaf of black, blank pages. Was it possible that for twenty-five years no American woman had had her likeness taken? "Submit a clear recent photo," as they say in job applications. But there was none, strange as it seemed considering the dominant role women are supposed to play in American life.

So I tried the experiment with men. The result was almost the same. Captain Ahab, Christopher Newman in *The American,* Babbitt, Elmer Gantry, Gatsby, Mac and Charley Anderson in Dos Passos, Jason in *The Sound and the Fury,* Colonel Sutpen in *Absalom, Absalom,*

This is the substance of a talk or talks given in Yugoslavia and England in the winter of 1960.

Flem and Mink Snopes, Studs Lonigan. After that, nothing, no one, except the Catholic priests of J. F. Powers, the bugler Prewitt in *From Here to Eternity,* and Henderson in *Henderson the Rain King.*

Someone might see this as a proof of the conformity of American life; there are no people any more, it might be claimed—only human vectors with acceleration and force. But in my experience this is simply not true. There are more people than ever before, at least in the sense of mutations in our national botany, and this is probably due to mobility—cross-fertilization. Take as an example a gangster who was in the slot-machine racket, decided to go straight and became a laundromat king, sent his daughter to Bennington, where she married a poet-in-residence or a professor of modern linguistic philosophy. There are three characters already sketched out in that sentence and all of them brand-new: the father, the daughter, and the son-in-law. Imagine what one of the old writers might have made of the wedding and the reception afterward at the 21 Club. The laundromat king or his equivalent is easy to meet in America; there are hundreds of him. Try teaching in a progressive college and interviewing the students' parents. And do not pretend that the laundromat king has no "inner life"; he is probably a Sunday painter, who has studied with Hans Hofman in Provincetown. What, for that matter, was the inner life of Monsieur Homais in *Madame Bovary?* People speak of the lack of tradition or of manners as having a bad effect on the American novel, but the self-made man is a far richer figure, from the novelist's point of view, than the man of inherited wealth, who is likely to be a mannered shadow.

The relations between parents and children (Turgenev's great theme) have never been so curious as in America now, where primitivism heads into decadence before it has time to turn around. America is full of Bazarovs but only Turgenev has described them. Nobody, as far as I know, has described an "action" painter, yet nearly everyone has met one. Nobody has done justice to the psychoanalyst, yet nearly everyone has gone to one. And what a wealth of material there is in that virgin field, what variety: the orthodox Freudian, the Horneyite, the Reichian, the Sullivanite ("interpersonal relations"), all the different kinds of revisionists, the lay analyst, the specialist in group analysis, the psychiatric social worker. Social workers themselves have become one of the major forces in American life, the real and absolute administrators of the lives of the poor, yet no one since Sinclair Lewis and Dos Passos has dared write of them, unless you count the young author, John Updike, in *The Poorhouse Farm,* who presents a single specimen and lays the story in the future. Imagine what Dickens would have done with this new army of beadles and the Mrs. Pardiggles behind them or what he would have done with the modern architect as Pecksniff, with the cant formula "Less is more." No serious writer since Dos Passos, so far as I know, has had a go at the government official, and the government official has not only multiplied but changed (like the social worker) since Dos Passos' time, producing many sub-varieties. And what about the foundation executive? Or the "behavioral scientist"? The fact is that the very forces and institutions that are the agents and promoters of conformity in America—bureaucracies public and private and the regimented "schools" and systems of healing and artistic creation—are themselves, through splits and cellular irritation, propagating an array of social types conforming to no previous standard, though when we look for names for them we are driven back, *faute de mieux,* on the old names: Pecksniff, Mrs. Gamp, Bazarov, Mrs. Pardiggle, Babbitt. When Peter Viereck, in a book of nonfiction, wanted to isolate a new kind of conformist intellectual he could think of nothing better to call him than "Babbitt Junior." It is as though a whole "culture" of plants and organisms had sprung into being and there were no scientists or latter-day Adams to name them.

This naming is very important, yet only two names in recent fiction have "stuck": Gulley Jimson (Joyce Cary) and Lucky Jim (Kingsley Amis). Some interest in character is still shown by writers in England, perhaps because it is an island and hence more conscious of itself. But even in England the great national portrait gallery that constituted the English novel is short of new acquisitions. The sense of character began to fade with D. H. Lawrence. After *Sons and Lovers,* we do not remember figures in Lawrence's books, except for a few short malicious sketches. There are hardly any people in Virginia Woolf (Mr. Ramsay in *To the Lighthouse* stands out) or in Forster or Elizabeth Bowen or Henry Green; they exist in Ivy Compton-Burnett but tend to blur together like her titles. Waugh has people, and so had Joyce Cary. You find them in the short stories of V. S. Pritchett and in the satires of Angus Wilson. But the last great creator of character in the English novel was Joyce. It is the same on the Continent. After Proust, a veil is drawn. You can speak of someone as a "regular Madame Verdurin" or a "Charlus," but from Gide, Sartre, Camus, no names emerge; the register is closed.

The meaning of this seems plain. The novel and the short story have lost interest in the social. Since the social has certainly not lost interest in itself (look at the popularity of such strange mirror-books as *The Lonely Crowd, The Organization Man, The Exurbanites, The Status Seekers*), what has happened must have occurred inside the novel and the short story—a technical or even techological crisis. An impasse has been reached within the art of fiction as a result of progress and experiment. You find a similar impasse in painting, where the portrait can no longer be painted and not because the artists do not know how to draw or get a likeness; they do. But they can no longer see a likeness as a work of art. In one sense, it is ridiculous to speak of progress in the arts (as though modern art were "better" than Rembrandt or Titian); in another sense, there *is* progress, an internal dynamic such as one finds in the processes of industry or in the biological process of aging. The arts have aged too, and it is impossible for them to "go back," just as it is impossible to recapture the youth or reinstitute a handicraft economy, like the one Ruskin dreamed of. These things are beyond our control and independent of our will. I, for instance, would like, more than anything else, to write like Tolstoy; I imagine that I still see something resembling the world Tolstoy saw. But my pen or my typewriter simply balks; it "sees" differently from me and records what to me, as a person, are distortions and angularities. Anyone who has read my work will be at a loss to find any connection with Tolstoy; to Tolstoy himself both I and my work would be anathema. I myself might reform, but my work never could; it could never "go straight," even if I were much more gifted than I am. Most novelists today, I suspect, would like to "go straight"; we are conscious of being twisted when we write. This is the self-consciousness, the squirming, of the form we work in; we are stuck in the phylogenesis of the novel.

The fictional experiments of the twentieth century went in two directions: sensibility and sensation. To speak very broadly, the experiments in the recording of sensibility were made in England (Virginia Woolf, Katherine Mansfield, Dorothy Richardson, Elizabeth Bowen, Forster), and America was the laboratory of sensation (Hemingway and his imitators, Dos Passos, Farrell). The novel of sensibility was feminine, and the novel of sensation was masculine. In Paris, there was a certain meeting and merging: Gertrude Stein (a robust recorder of the data of sensibility) influenced and encouraged Hemingway; Joyce, who experimented in both directions, influenced nearly everyone. The sensibility tendency today is found chiefly in such minor English writers as Henry Green and William Sansom; in America, it is represented by Katharine Anne Porter, Eudora Welty, Jean Stafford, and Carson McCullers. The masculine novel of sensation, more admired always in Europe than at home, seems to have arrived at the Beat Generation, via Caldwell, Dashiell Hammett, James M. Cain, Raymond Chandler; its attraction toward violence propelled it naturally toward the crime story. The effect of these two tendencies on the subject matter of the novel was identical. Sensation and sensibility are the poles of each other, and both have the effect of abolishing the social. Sensibility, like violent action, annihilates the sense of character.

Beginning with our own. In violence, we forget who we are, just as we forget who we are when engaged in sheer perception. Immersed in a picture, an effect of light, or a landscape, we forget ourselves; we are "taken out of ourselves"; in the same way, we forget ourselves in the dentist's chair. We are not conscious of our personality. In sensation, we are all more or less alike. Heat, cold, hunger, thirst, pain are experienced by man, not men. And sensibility is not a refinement of sensation; the sense of blue or green made on our retina is more finely discriminated in an art critic than it is in the average man or the color-blind person, but no useful division, humanly speaking, could be made between those, say, who saw turquoise as green and those who saw it as blue. The retina is not the seat of character. Nor are the sexual organs, even though they differ from person to person. Making love, we are all more alike than we are when we are talking or acting. In the climax of the sexual act, moreover, we forget ourselves; that is commonly felt to be one of its recommendations. Sex annihilates identity, and the space given to sex in contemporary novels is an avowal of the absence of character. There are no "people" in *Lady Chatterley's Lover,* unless possibly the husband, who is impotent. To cite the laundromat king again, the moment of orgasm would not be the best moment for the novelist to seize upon to show his salient traits; on the other hand, to show him in an orgone box (i.e., in the frame of an idea) would be a splendid notion. Similarly, the perambulating sensibility of Mrs. Dalloway, her quivering film of perception, cannot fix for us Mrs. Dalloway as a person; she remains a palpitant organ, like the heroine of a pornographic novel. The character I remember best from Virginia Woolf is Mr. Ramsay in *To the Lighthouse,* a man who lacks the fine perceptions of the others; i.e., from the point of view of sensibility he is impotent, without erectile aesthetic tissue.

Sensation and sensibility are at their height in the child; its thin, tender membrane of perception is constantly being stabbed by objects, words, and events that it does not understand. In lieu of understanding, the child "notices." Think of the first sections of *A Portrait of the Artist as a Young Man* and of Aunt Dante's hairbrushes (why was she called Dante?) and the quarrel about Parnell (who was Parnell?) at the Christmas dinner table. Or the beginning of *Dr. Zhivago,* where the child Yury, taken to his mother's funeral, looks out the window at the cabbages, wrinkled and blue with cold, in the winter fields. Yury, being a child, cannot comprehend the important event that has happened to him (death), but his eye takes in the shivering cabbages. Everyone experiences something like this in moments of intense grief or public solemnity, such as funerals; feelings, distracted from their real causes, attach themselves arbitrarily to sights, smells, and sounds. But a child passes a good part of his life in this attentive state of detachment.

Now two characteristics of the child are that he cannot act (to any purpose) and he cannot talk (expressively); hence he is outside, dissociated. And it is just this state, of the dissociated outsider, that is at the center of modern literature of sensibility and sensation alike. Camus' *The Stranger* or *The Outsider* begins with the hero's going to his mother's deathbed and being unable to summon up the appropriate emotions or phrases.

It is modern but it is not new. The inability to say the appropriate thing or to feel the appropriate thing, combined with a horrible faculty of *noticing,* is an almost clinical trait in the character of Julien Sorel and in most of the Stendhalian heroes. Tolstoy was a master of the tragicomedy of inappropriate feelings, gestures, and sensations. Take the first chapter of *Anna Karenina,* where Stepan Oblonsky, who has been unfaithful to his wife with the French governess, finds a foolish smile spreading over his features when she taxes him with it—a *smile* of all things. He cannot forgive himself that awful, inadvertent smile (he ascribes it to a "reflex"), which causes her to shut herself up in her room and declare that all is over. Vronsky's toothache, near the end of *Anna Karenina,* as it were dunce-caps the climax; it is the distracted intrusion of the commonplace into a drama of tragic passion. Anna has killed herself, and Vronsky is on the train, going off to the Serbo-Turkish war as an "heroic volunteer" with a squadron equipped at his own expense; his face is drawn with suffering—and with the ache in his big tooth, which makes it almost impossible for him to speak. But "all at once a different pain, not an ache but an inner trouble, that set his whole being in anguish, made him for an instant forget his toothache." He has "suddenly remembered *her,*" as he has last seen her mangled body exposed on a table in the railway shed. And he ceases to feel his toothache and begins to sob. At every station the train is seen off by patriotic society ladies with nosegays for the heroic volunteers, and these flowers, like the toothache, are ridiculous and painful—beside the point.

The point, however, is there, inescapably so (the corpse in the railway shed is more cruelly alive than the toothache), and this is the difference between Tolstoy (Stendhal too) and the fragmented impressionism of twentieth-century literature, where the real world is broken up into disparate painterly images out of focus and therefore hypnotic and trancelike. The world of twentieth-century sensibility, in contrast to that of Tolstoy, is a world in slow motion, a world which, however happy it may seem, is a world of paralyzed grief, in which little irrelevant things, things that do not belong, are noticed or registered on the film of consciousness, exactly as they are at a funeral service or by a bored child in church.

In the modern novel of sensibility the shimmer of consciousness occupies the whole field of vision. Happenings are broken down into tiny discrete sensory impressions, recalling pointillism or the treatment of light in Monet. The novel of sensation is less refined and seemingly more "factual": "It was hot"; " 'Give me a drink,' I said." But these too are the *disjecta membra* of consciousness passing across a primitive perceptual screen. A child cannot talk, and the modern novel of sensation, like that of sensibility, is almost mute; these rolls of film are silent, with occasional terse flashes of dialogue, like subtitles. The only form of action open to a child is to break something or strike someone, its mother or another child; it cannot cause things to happen in the world. This is precisely the situation of the hero of the novel of sensation; violence becomes a substitute for action. In the novel of sensibility, nothing happens; as people complain, there is no plot.

Once these discoveries had been made, however, in the recording of the perceptual field (i.e., of pure subjectivity), the novel could not ignore them; there was no turning back to the objectivity of Tolstoy or the rational demonstrations of Proust. The "objective" novel of Sarraute, Robbe-Grillet, and Butor is simply a factual treatment of the data of consciousness, which are presented like clues in a detective story to the events that the reader guesses are taking place. The very notion of character is ruled out. One way, however, remains open to the novelist who is interested in character (which means in human society)—a curious back door. That is the entry found by Joyce in *Ulysses,* where by a humorous stratagem character is shown, as it were, inside out, from behind the screen of consciousness. The interior monologue every human being conducts with himself, *sotto voce,* is used to create a dramatic portrait. There is no question but that Mr. Bloom and Molly are characters, quite as much as the characters of Dickens or any of the old novelists—not mere bundles of vagrant sensory impressions but articulated wholes. Their soliloquies are really half of a dialogue—a continuous argument with society, whose answers or objections can be inferred. Mr. Bloom and Molly are pathetically social, gregarious,

worldly, and lonely: misunderstood. This sense of being
the victim of a misunderstanding dominates *Finnegans
Wake,* where the hero is Everybody—the race itself.
Nothing could be more vocal than these books of Joyce:
talk, talk, talk. *Finnegans Wake* is a real babel of voices,
from the past, from literature, from the house next door
and the street; even the river Liffey chatters. We would
know Mr. Bloom anywhere by his voice, the inmost Mr.
Bloom; the same with Molly. Joyce was a master mimic
of the voice of conscience, and Mr. Bloom and Molly
are genuine imitations. This blind artist was the great
ventriloquist of the novel. A sustained power of mimicry
is the secret of all creators of character; Joyce had it
while Virginia Woolf, say, did not. That is why Joyce
was able to give shape and body—in short, singularity,
definition—to the senseless data of consciousness.

The notion that life is senseless, a tale told by an
idiot—the under-theme of twentieth-century literature—
is affirmed again by Faulkner in *The Sound and the Fury.*
Yet here, as in *Ulysses,* characters appear from the mists
of their own reveries and sensations: the idiot Benjy,
Jason, Dilsey, the Negro cook. And a plot, even, is in-
dicated for the reader to piece together from clues
dropped here and there: the story of Caddy and the
castration of Benjy and Quentin's suicide. The materiali-
zation of plot and character prove that there *is* being,
after all, beyond the arbitrary flux of existence. Following Joyce and Faulkner, the imitation-from-within became almost standard practice for writers who were impatient with the fragmented impressionist novel and who
had assimilated nonetheless some of its techniques. To
use the technique of impressionism to create something
quite different—a character study—seems the manifest
intention of Joyce Cary in *The Horse's Mouth,* where the
author, as it were, impersonates the eye of Gulley Jimson, an old reprobate painter down on his luck; the dancing, broken surface is only a means, like the muttering
of an inner dialogue, to show the man in action, inces-
santly painting in his mind's eye as he boozily peregrinates

the docks and streets. Something very similar is John Updike's *The Poorhouse Farm,* which is seen through the resentful hyperopic eye of an old man sitting on the porch of a county poorhouse. The sign of this kind of writing, the mark of its affiliation with the pure impressionist or stream-of-consciousness novel, is that when you start the book you do not know where you are. It takes you quite a few pages to get your bearings, just as if you were bumping along inside a sack in some fairy story; then you awake to the fact that the consciousness you have been thrust into is named Benjy and is feebleminded or is a criminal old painter with a passion for William Blake's poetry or a charity patient whose eyesight, owing to the failing muscles of old age, bends and distorts everything in the immediate foreground and can only focus clearly on what is far off. Once you know where you are, you can relax and study your surroundings, though you must watch out for sudden, disorienting jolts and jerks—an indication that the character is in movement, colliding or interacting with objective reality.

The reader, here, as in *Ulysses,* is restricted to a narrow field of vision or to several narrow fields in succession. Now something comparable happens in recent books that, on the surface, seem to owe very little to the stream-of-consciousness tradition and to take no interest in the mechanics of perception or the field of vision as such. I mean such books as *Augie March, Henderson the Rain King, The Catcher in the Rye, Lolita,* and two of my own novels, *The Groves of Academe* and *A Charmed Life.* These books are impersonations, ventriloquial acts; the author, like some prankster on the telephone, is speaking in an assumed voice—high or deep, hollow or falsetto, but in any case not his own. He is imitating the voice of Augie or of Holden Caulfield and the book is written in Augie's or Holden's "style." The style is the man (or the boy), and the author, pretending to be Augie or Holden or Humbert Humbert, remains "in character" throughout the book, unless he shifts to another style, that is, to another character. These books, in short, are dramatic monologues or series of dramatic monologues. The reader, tuned in, is left in no doubt as to where he is physically, and yet in many of these books he finds himself puzzled by the very vocal consciousness he has entered: is it good or bad, impartial or biased? Can it be trusted as Huck Finn or Marcel or David Copperfield could be trusted? He senses the author, cramped inside the character like a contortionist in a box, and suspects (often rightly) some trick. In short, it is not all straight shooting, as it was with the old novelists.

This is not a defect, yet it points to the defects of the method, which can be summed up as a lack of straightforwardness. There is something burglarious about these silent entries into a private and alien consciousness. Or so I feel when I do it myself. It is exhilarating but not altogether honest to make believe I am a devious red-haired man professor with bad breath and bits of toilet paper on his face, to talk under my breath his sibilant, vindictive thought-language and draw his pale lips tightly across my teeth. "So *this* is how the world looks to a man like that!" I can say to myself, awestruck, and so, I expect, John Updike, twenty-five years old, must have felt when he discovered what it felt like to be an old pauper with loosened eye-muscles sitting on a poorhouse porch. But I cannot know, really, what it feels like to be a vindictive man professor, any more than a young man can know what it is to be an old man or Faulkner can know what it is to be a feebleminded adult who has had his balls cut off. All fictions, of course, are impersonations, but it seems to me somehow less dubious to impersonate the outside of a person, say Mrs. Micawber with her mysterious "I will never leave Mr. Micawber," than to claim to know what it feels like to *be* Mrs. Micawber. These impersonations, moreover, are laborious; to come at a character circuitously, by a tour de force, means spending great and sometimes disproportionate pains on the method of entry. I read somewhere that Salinger spent ten years writing *The Catcher in the Rye;* that was eight years too long. Granted, the book is a feat, but it compels admiration more as a feat than as a novel, like the performance of a one-armed violinist or any other curiosity. This could not be said of *Huckleberry Finn;* Mark Twain's imitation of Huck's language is never, so to speak, the drawing card. In the cases of Salinger, Updike, myself, one wonders whether the care expended on the mechanics of the imitation, on getting the right detail, vocabulary, and so on, does not constitute a kind of advertisement for the author, eliciting such responses as "Think of the work that went into it!" or "Imagine a twenty-five-year-old being able to take off an old man like that!" One is reminded of certain young actors whose trademark is doing character parts, or, vice versa, of certain old actresses whose draw can be summed up in the sentence "You would never guess she was sixty."

Yet you might say that it was a fine thing for a well-paid writer in his twenties to know from the inside what it was like to be an aged charity patient. Very democratic. True, and this is a real incentive for the novelist of the twentieth century. The old authors identified with the hero or the heroine, a sympathetic figure whose dreams and desires resembled the author's own. *"Madame Bovary, c'est moi,"* said Flaubert, and no doubt there was quite a lot of Madame Bovary in him or of him in Madame Bovary. Allowing for the differences of circumstance and intellect, he could have been Emma Bovary; the stretch of imagination to encompass her circumstances and her intellect was a great step, of course, in the democratization of the novel, and the naturalists, English and French, pushed further in this direction, with their studies of servant girls, factory operatives, and of the submerged poor in general. Even James tried it with his poor little anarchist, Hyacinthe Robinson. Yet here, as in Flaubert, there is still the idea of a hero or a heroine—mute inglorious Cinderellas who never went to the ball; what separates the author from the hero or the heroine is fate or social destiny. Their souls are not alien. But for the writer today (the writer who has any interest in character) it has become almost obligatory not merely to traverse social barriers but to invade the privacy of a soul so foreign or so foetal as to seem beyond grasp. Take *Ulysses*. Molly Bloom is not a soulmate of Joyce's or a sister under the skin. She is as far removed from Joyce as you could get and still remain human—the antipodes. Mr. Bloom is closer, but he is not Joyce as he might have been if he were Jewish, an advertising canvasser, and married to Molly. He is an independent, sovereign world to which Joyce has managed to gain access. There is no doctrine of "sympathies" or a-touch-of-nature-makes-the-whole-world-kin underlying *Ulysses*. Or underlying *The Sound and the Fury*, where Faulkner explores the inner life of the mental defective Benjy—his own, you might say, diametrical opposite. Much of modern literature might be defined as the search for one's own diametrical opposite, which is then used as the point-of-view. The parallel would be if Dickens had tried to write *David Copperfield* from within the sensibility of Uriah Heep or *Oliver Twist* through the impressions of Fagin.

Difficulty alone (though it always exercises a charm) does not explain the appeal of such enterprises for modern writers. There is something else—a desire to comprehend, which seems to be growing stronger as the world itself becomes more incomprehensible and dubious. The older writers, when they sought their characters from among the poor and the obscure, assumed that there was a common humanity and were concerned to show this. But it is that very assumption that is being tested, tried out, by the writers of today when they start examining their own opposites. I will give an illustration from my own work to show what I mean, rather than presume to speak for others.

When I first had the idea of the book called *The Groves of Academe*, it presented itself as a plot with a single character at the center. An unsavory but intelligent professor who teaches modern literature in an experimental college is told that his contract will not be renewed for reasons not specified but because in fact he is a trouble-maker; whereupon, he proceeds to demonstrate his ability to make trouble by launching a demagogic campaign for reappointment, claiming that he is being dismissed for having been a Communist and parading himself as the victim of a witch-hunt. This claim is totally false, but it is successful, for he has gauged very well the atmosphere of a liberal college during the period of anti-Communist hysteria that reached a climax in Senator McCarthy. No one in that liberal college stops to inquire whether he has really been a Communist because everyone is too preoccupied with defending his right to have been one and still remain a teacher; even the college president, knowing (who better?) that politics has nothing to do with the professor's being dropped from the faculty, yields as a professional liberal to this blackmail. Now the normal way of telling this story would be from the outside or from the point of view of one of the professor's sympathizers. But I found I had no interest in telling it that way; to me, the interest lay in trying to see it from the professor's point of view and mouthing it in the clichés and the hissing jargon of his vocabulary. That is, I wanted to know just how it felt to be raging inside the skin of a Henry Mulcahy and to learn how, among other things, he arrived at a sense of self-justification and triumphant injury that allowed him, as though he had been issued a license, to use any means to promote his personal cause, how he manipulated and combined an awareness of his own undesirability with the modern myth of the superior man hated and envied by mediocrity. To do this, naturally, I had to use every bit of Mulcahy there was in me, and there was not very much: I am not a paranoid, nor a liar, nor consumed with hatred, nor a man, for that matter. But this very fact was the stimulus. If I could understand Mulcahy, if I could make myself *be* Mulcahy, it would get me closer to the mystery, say, of Hitler and of all the baleful demagogic figures of modern society whom I could not imagine being. There was no thought of *"Tout comprendre, c'est pardonner"* or of offering a master-key to public events like *Darkness at Noon*. What I was after was something much more simple, naïve, and childlike: the satisfaction of the curiosity we all feel when we read in the paper of some crime we cannot imagine committing, like the case of the man who insured his mother-in-law at the airport and then planted a bomb in the plane she was taking. Certain crimes, certain characters, in their impudence or awfulness, have the power of making us feel *bornés,* and in a sense I wanted to tiptoe into the interior of Mulcahy like a peasant coming into a palace. The question was the same as between the peasant and the king: did we belong to the same species or not? The book is not an answer, but an experiment, an assaying.

There is an element of the private game, even of the private joke, in this kind of writing—a secret and comic relation between the author and his character. An arcane laughter, too internal for the reader to hear, quietly shakes such books; the points, the palpable hits (inspired turns of phrases, *trouvailles* of vocabulary) may altogether escape the reader's notice. Indeed, it sometimes happens that the reader is quite unaware of what the author is doing and complains that the style is full of clichés, when that, precisely, is the point. Or the glee of the hidden author may produce uncanny noises, such as the giggle or whinny overheard sometimes in *Lolita* testifying to who-knows-what indecorous relations between the author and Humbert Humbert. Joyce salted his work with private jokes, hints, and references that no one but *he* could be expected to enjoy, yet with Joyce it added to the savor. Lesser writers (or at least I) find themselves constrained by the naturalistic requirements of the method, the duty to keep a straight face, stay in character, speak in an assumed voice, hollow or falsetto, as though in a game that has gone on too long and that no one knows how to stop. There are moments when one would like to drop the pretense of being Mulcahy and go on with the business of the novel.

To return to the question of character. What do we

mean when we say there are "real people" in a book?
If you examine the works of Jane Austen, who, everyone
agrees, was a creator of characters, you will find that
the "real people" in her books are not so often the heroes
and heroines as the minor characters: Lady Catherine
de Bourgh and Mr. Collins, Mr. and Mrs. Bennet, Lady
Bertram, poor Miss Bates, Emma's friend Harriet, the
timorous and valetudinarian Mr. Woodhouse. These beings are much more thoroughly and wonderfully themselves than the heroes and heroines are able to be; the
reason for this is, I think, that they are comic.

Or turn to *Ulysses*. Who would deny that Stephen
Dedalus, a straight character, seems less "real" than Mr.
Bloom and Molly, less "real" than his father, Mr.
Dedalus? In what does this "reality" consist? In the in-
corrigibility and changelessness of the figure. Villains may
reform, heroes and heroines may learn their lesson, like
Emma or Elizabeth or Mr. Darcy, or grow into the author, like Stephen Dedalus and David Copperfield, but a
Lady Catherine de Bourgh or a Molly Bloom or a Mr.
Dedalus, regardless of resolutions, cannot reform or
change, cannot be other than they are. Falstaff is a species
of eternity; that is why the Hostess' description of his
death is so poignantly sad, far sadder than the pretty
death of Ophelia, for Falstaff, according to the laws of
his creation, should not die. This was Queen Elizabeth's
opinion too when she demanded his resurrection and
Shakespeare obliged with *The Merry Wives of Windsor*.
"Mortal men, mortal men," Falstaff sighs speciously, but
he himself is an immortal, an everlasting, like Mr. and
Mrs. Micawber who, when last heard of, were still going
strong in Australia. The same with Mrs. Gamp, Pecksniff, Stepan Oblonsky, Monsieur Homais, Stepan Tro-
fimovitch, old Karamazov. Real characterization, I think,
is seldom accomplished outside of comedy or without the
fixative of comedy; the stubborn pride of Mr. Darcy, the
prejudice of Elizabeth, the headstrongness of Emma. A
comic character, contrary to accepted belief, is likely to
be more complicated and enigmatic than a hero or a

heroine, fuller of surprises and turnabouts; Mr. Micawber, for instance, can find the most unexpected ways of
being himself; so can Mr. Woodhouse or the Master of
the Marshalsea. It is a sort of resourcefulness.

What we recognize as reality in these figures is their
implacable resistance to change; they are what perdures
or remains—the monoliths or plinths of the world. Pierre
in *War and Peace* seems more real than Levin, his opposite number in *Anna Karenina*. This is because Pierre
is fat—fat and awkward and wears a funny-looking green
civilian hat at the Battle of Borodino, like a sign of his
irreducible innocent stoutness. Thanks to a streak of
cruelty or sarcastic sharpness in Tolstoy, most of his
heroes and heroines are not spared a satirical glance that
picks out their weak points. Vronsky's bald spot, Prince
Andrei's small white hands, the heavy step of the Prin-
cess Marya. They live as characters because Tolstoy is
always conscious of their limitations, just as he is with
his comic figures; he does not forget that Anna is a society woman and Vronsky a smart cavalry officer—types
that in real life he disapproved of and even detested.

The comic element is the incorrigible element in every
human being; the capacity to learn, from experience or
instruction, is what is forbidden to all comic creations
and to what is comic in you and me. This capacity to
learn is the prerogative of the hero or the heroine:
Prince Hal as opposed to Falstaff. The principle of growth
in human beings is as real, of course (though possibly
not so common), as the principle of eternity or inertia
represented by the comic; it is the subjective as opposed
to the objective. When we identify ourselves with the hero
of a story, we are following him with all our hopes, i.e.,
with our subjective conviction of human freedom; on the
comic characters we look with despair, in which, though,
there is a queer kind of admiration—we really, I believe,
admire the comic characters *more* than we do the hero
or the heroine, because of their obstinate power to do-it-
again, combined with a total lack of self-consciousness or
shame. But it is the hero or the heroine whose fate we

feel suspense for, whom we blush for when they make a mistake; we put ourselves in their place from the very first pages, from the minute we make their acquaintance. We do not have to *know* the hero or the heroine to be on their side; not even a name is necessary. We are pulling for them if they are called "K." or "he." This mechanism of identification with the hero is very odd and seems to rest, almost, on *lack* of knowledge. If a book or story begins, "He took the train that night," we are surer that "he" is the hero (i.e., our temporary double) than if it begins, "Richard Col took the five forty-five Thursday night." Or "Count Karenin seated himself in a first-class carriage on the Moscow-Petersburg express." We would wait to hear more about this "Richard Col" or "Count Karenin" before depositing our sympathies with him. This throws an interesting light on the question of character.

In the modern novel there is little suspense. No one reads *Ulysses* or *Finnegans Wake* or *The Sound and the Fury* or *Mrs. Dalloway* for the sake of the story, to find out what is going to happen to the hero or the heroine. The chief plot interest in these books is to try to find out what happened before the book started: what was in that letter the chicken scratched up? what had Earwicker done in Phoenix Park? why does Benjy get so excited every time he is taken near the golf course? what is biting Stephen ("agenbite of inwit")? who, really, has been Clarissa Dalloway? The absence of suspense means that the cord of identification between the reader and the hero has deliberately been cut. Or put it a different way: the reader, as I have said, wakes up in a foreign consciousness, a bundle of impressions, not knowing where he is. The first reaction is a mild panic, an attack of claustrophobia; far from the reader's identifying, say, with Stephen at the outset of *Ulysses,* his whole wish is to fight his way out of Stephen into the open world, in order to discover where Stephen is and what is going on. And even when these fears have been quieted (Stephen is in a tower; he lives with Buck Mulligan, a medical student; his mother has just died), new fears surge up and always of a locative character, so that the reader is put in the position of a perpetual outsider, hearing what Stephen hears, seeing what Stephen sees but failing to get the drift often, asking bewildered questions: "Where am I?" "Who is talking?" "What's up?" An anxiety about location (the prime clinical symptom in the reader of the modern novel) precludes interest in direction; in any case, the end is foreordained: nothing can happen to Stephen but to become Joyce. Stephen is neither subject nor object, neither hero nor comedian, but the bombarded center of a perceptual all-out attack; in this sense, *Ulysses* is a scientific study in the logistics of personality. In the laboratory of the modern novel, the author *qua* author (not *qua* character) is the spot-lit master-figure. And in science the only hero can be the white-coated scientist; the rest is data. The difference can be felt by a comparison with Proust. Proust's Marcel is still a hero, followed by the reader with suspense, to learn what will happen with his grandmother, what will happen with Gilberte, what will happen with Albertine—something more *can* happen to him than to become Proust. Marcel is a pure subject, despite the attention he pays to studying and analyzing his reactions; if the book is, in part, a reconstruction of anterior events, it is Marcel himself, not just the reader, who is trying to find out what actually took place before the book started, and this quest for certainty is itself a hero's goal.

In the old novels, there was a continual fluctuating play between the hero and the "characters," that is, between the world as we feel it to be subjectively and the world as we know it as observers. As subjects, we all live in suspense, from day to day, from hour to hour; in other words, we are the hero of our own story. We cannot believe that it is finished, that we are "finished," even though we may say so; we expect another chapter, another installment, tomorrow or next week. In moments of despair, we look on ourselves leadenly as objects; we see

ourselves, our lives, as someone else might see them
and may even be driven to kill ourselves if the separation,
the "knowledge," seems sufficiently final. Our view of
others, on the contrary, cannot but be objective and
therefore tinged with a sad sense of comedy. Others are
to us like the "characters" of fiction, eternal and incorrigible; the surprises they give us turn out in the end to
have been predictable—unexpected variations on the
theme of being themselves, of the *principio individua-
tionis*. But it is just this principle that we cannot see in
ourselves. What is happening in modern literature is a
peculiar reversal of roles: we try to show the object as
subject and the subject as object. That is, can I be inside
Professor Mulcahy and outside me? The answer is I
cannot; no one can. There can only be one subject, ourselves, one hero or heroine. The existentialist paradox—
that we are subjects for ourselves and objects for others
—cannot be resolved by technical virtuosity. The best
efforts, far from mastering the conundrum, merely result
in the creation of characters—Benjy, Jason, Molly, Mr.
Bloom, and so on—who are more or less "successful"
in exactly the old sense, more or less "realized," concrete, objectively existent. Choirs of such characters make
up the modern novel. What has been lost, however, in
the continuing experiment is the power of the author to
speak in his own voice or through the undisguised voice
of an alter ego, the hero, at once a known and an unknown, a bearer of human freedom. It would seem, moreover, that there was a kind of symbiosis between the hero
and the "characters," that you could not have the one
without the others or the others without the one. The
loss of the hero upset a balance of nature in the novel,
and the languishing of the "characters" followed. Certainly the common world that lies between the contemporary reader and the contemporary author remains un-
explored, almost undescribed, just as queer and empty a
place as Dickens' world would be if he had spent eight

years recording the impressions of Fagin or the sensory
data received by Uriah Heep in the slithery course of a
morning's walk.

March, 1961